Hidden Rhythms of Teams

For readers who want to understand the hidden logic of how teams actually work, this book challenges the myth of the perfectly aligned, "optimized" culture and instead reveals how tension and conflict make real teams resilient.

Drawing on eighteen months of immersive observation inside four small firms, Eric R. Kushins offers a rare, firsthand look at teams in action. He uncovers how effective team cultures emerge, shift, and sustain themselves over time. Readers gain new conceptual tools for recognizing how relationships, rituals, and routines shape organizational performance, along with practical strategies for managing the cultural cycle of stability, crisis, and growth.

Culture is not a program to be rolled out. It is a performance lived every day. By understanding the dynamics that govern team interaction, leaders can better coordinate work, manage tension, and build organizations capable of navigating change. *Hidden Rhythms of Teams* is an essential guide for executives, HR leaders, consultants, entrepreneurs, family business owners, and MBA students seeking to build organizations that perform, adapt, and endure.

Eric R. Kushins is Associate Professor of Management at Berry College's Campbell School of Business and holds a dual PhD in Sociology and Management from Rutgers University. He is a frequent media contributor and leads executive education programs across the Southeast US.

Hidden Rhythms of Teams

The Cultural Routines That Shape Business Success

Eric R. Kushins

Routledge
Taylor & Francis Group
NEW YORK AND LONDON

Designed cover image: Getcovers

First published 2027
by Routledge
605 Third Avenue, New York, NY 10158

and by Routledge
4 Park Square, Milton Park, Abingdon, Oxon, OX14 4RN

Routledge is an imprint of the Taylor & Francis Group, an informa business

Library of Congress Cataloging-in-Publication Data
Names: Kushins, Eric R. author
Title: hidden rhythms of teams : the cultural routines that shape business success / Eric R. Kushins.
Description: New York, NY : Routledge, 2027. | Includes bibliographical references and index. |
Identifiers: LCCN 2026016168 (print) | LCCN 2026016169 (ebook) | ISBN 9781041315803 hardback | ISBN 9781041315780 paperback | ISBN 9781003779803 ebook
Subjects: LCSH: Teams in the workplace | Success in business
Classification: LCC HD66 .K877 2027 (print) | LCC HD66 (ebook)
LC record available at https://lccn.loc.gov/2026016168
LC ebook record available at https://lccn.loc.gov/2026016169

ISBN: 9781041315803 (hbk)
ISBN: 9781041315780 (pbk)
ISBN: 9781003779803 (ebk)

DOI: 10.4324/9781003779803

Typeset in Sabon
by codeMantra

Contents

Prelude

Chapter 1

Rethinking Culture at Work

I awoke as a hot dog in a bun. It was now 6:30 a.m. and Penelope had been moving about the house for over an hour, tending to her morning routines. She aggressively rang a bell from the kitchen and began singing her "Good Morning" song, its words and a melody different each day. Today's version took on the cadence of a hymn. "Good morning, my children, rise…" Five guys in their twenties, scattered around me in the room, groaned awake. One jokingly whimpered for our shared amusement, "Pleeease stop… pleeease just shut up."

I didn't realize before joining Rolling Hills as a farmhand that the air mattress I brought had a small hole in it. In this living room, converted into men's sleeping quarters, two twin, shabby-looking spring mattresses sat alongside a collection of airbeds and sleeping bags strewn across the floor. The spring mattresses, owned by Penelope, were claimed by the longest-tenured volunteers, even though house rules required all farmhands to bring their own sleep gear. Each morning, I woke up practically on the floor, the mattress sagging beneath me with inflated sections gathered on either side.

To better fit in with the team, I chose not to fix the leak or buy a new mattress. Doing so would have marked me as someone who would seem to care about quality sleep or was frivolous with money. Instead, I learned to tolerate the physical discomfort over the next eighteen months at Rolling Hills.

What appears to be a simple morning routine, marked by shared groans at early morning singing, a collective sense of infantilization, an unspoken hierarchy of bed allocation, and tacit rules about how to fit in, reveals something deeper. The rhythm of recognition, social ordering, and attunement did not come from formal rules, but from improvised norms developed over time through ongoing interaction, communication, and negotiation within the team. Coordination and motivation arose through shared practices, not managerial command.

DOI: 10.4324/9781003779803-2

How did I end up committing to a year and a half of stiff necks and aching backs, returning to a dorm room-style living arrangement where a loud bell marked the start of each day, breakfast was day-old pastries, and farm work—from collecting eggs and digging carrots to harvesting kale, picking grape tomatoes, and hauling compost to the goats—was divvied each morning? I took on this life at Rolling Hills, along with work in three other small businesses, to understand what enables teams to function and endure. Working alongside others, sharing their routines, and absorbing the rhythms of daily coordination through ethnographic immersion offered a ground-level view of teamwork that no survey, interview, or management framework could match.

Where Culture Really Lives

Most leadership and management books focus on the individual. When teams struggle, the explanation often sounds familiar. The leader lacks vision, employees resist change, communication breaks down, or cognitive biases interfere. These accounts are appealing because they promise clear solutions. If we coach the leader, train the employee, or reframe the problem, improvement should follow.

And yet, anyone who has spent time inside a business knows this story rarely holds. Leaders with strong intentions fail to shift entrenched norms. Training programs generate enthusiasm that quickly fades. Culture initiatives stall, even when everyone agrees they matter. These failures are not accidental. They stem from a category error whereby culture is treated as primarily psychological rather than social.

For decades, leadership research and popular management writing have leaned heavily on psychological explanations to understand organizational behavior. Motivation, personality traits, emotional intelligence, and individual decision-making dominate accounts of success or failure at work. These perspectives are not wrong, but they are incomplete. Culture does not reside inside people's heads. It exists between them, embedded in interaction, roles, histories, power relations, and shared meanings that accumulate over time. To understand the persistence of friction, the emergence of coordination, and the endurance of inequities, we must redirect our analytic lens from psychology to sociology.

A sociological approach foregrounds interaction rather than intention. It asks how people relate to one another in patterned ways, how expectations solidify through repeated encounters, and how power circulates through everyday practices. Where psychology often asks, "What is this individual thinking or feeling?" sociology asks, "What social situation are they embedded in, and what does that situation make possible or constrain?"

This reorientation guided my approach in this book. Rather than relying solely on interviews or retrospective accounts, I worked alongside teams in real time, sharing their daily routines. That immersion provided an unusually clear view of the messy, contradictory realities of teamwork, including the humor, fatigue, competition, dysfunction, and creativity through which team culture is produced.

This approach reflects more than academic curiosity. Before starting my career in higher education, I spent several years working alongside small business owners, helping them develop and refine their business concepts and expand their operations, client bases, and reach. That experience led me to pursue doctoral training in both sociology and management to better understand how teams and organizations coordinate, adapt, and endure. For more than a decade, I have served as a business school professor, conducting research on small businesses and family firms while working regularly with business leaders across industries as a consultant and executive education instructor. My work bridges scholarship and practice. These experiences strengthened my conviction that the most consequential dynamics of performance are rarely captured in strategy documents or leadership slogans. They unfold instead within teams.

Culture as Performance

One of the central findings in this book is that teams move through three recurring cultural performances as they work: routine stability, routine crisis, and routine growth. Each performance organizes behavior in distinct ways, elevates different voices, and reshapes what counts as appropriate action. Teams do not abandon culture when conditions change. They shift cultural gears. They draw from a broad repertoire of shared knowledge and apply it collectively to the situation at hand. What appears inconsistent from the outside is often a skilled, situational response to changing demands.

This insight departs sharply from how culture is typically discussed in business scholarship and practice. Most models treat culture as a single, stable set of shared values or norms that leaders should align, reinforce, or redesign. In contrast, this book shows that culture is situational and performative. The same team may rely on collaboration and flexibility during routine work, centralize authority during moments of crisis, and tolerate ambiguity and experimentation during periods of growth. These shifts are not cultural failures or contradictions. They are patterned responses to changing organizational conditions. Focusing on performance rather than assuming unity allows leaders to see culture where it lives—in teams as they navigate stability, crisis, and growth.

Why Small Businesses

Small businesses are an especially powerful context for studying work teams because everyday coordination is more visible. In small firms, teams are tight, hierarchies are compressed, and members encounter one another repeatedly across formal and informal settings. Rather than relying on formal procedures or fixed playbooks, teams coordinate through shared understandings built over time. As a result, the subtle processes that sustain coordination, generate conflict, and produce meaning are harder to hide. Everyday rituals, unspoken rules, micro-inequalities, and symbolic power dynamics become observable in real time.

I show how small businesses function as social laboratories where teamwork performances can be examined with ethnographic depth. In these settings, culture is not a slogan or a values statement handed down from leadership. It is enacted, contested, and made durable through repeated interaction as teams respond to changing conditions.

At the same time, studying small businesses does not limit the relevance of these findings. The social mechanisms uncovered in small firms are not unique to them but are foundational to organizations of all sizes and to collective life more broadly. Although this book focuses on work teams, the logics it describes recur wherever people must coordinate action over time, from nuclear families and little league teams to classrooms, military units, faith communities, volunteer organizations, and civic groups. Larger organizations and international teams are built from the same interactional elements of meetings, handoffs, negotiations, trust repairs, shared histories, and meaning-making moments. What changes with scale is not the logic of social life but the ease with which it can be observed. By tracing how team rhythms emerge in small firms, where misalignments surface quickly and repairs come into view, we gain analytic leverage on how similar dynamics operate in large, complex organizations, professional service firms, and globally distributed teams.

This book's contribution, therefore, is not a theory of "small business culture" but a portable framework for understanding how social order is produced and sustained across organizations of varying size and national context. Small businesses make visible the social infrastructure that enables collective work everywhere.

Seeing Culture In Action

Hidden Rhythms of Teams advances a simple but powerful claim that performance is driven not primarily by individual leaders, formal strategy, or a designed culture but by the rhythms teams create together in everyday work.

Teams are where organizational life unfolds. This is a basic sociological truth. People learn what matters, what to value, how to act, and what counts as good work through the routines, relationships, and practical problem-solving of their teams. While much business writing still treats culture as something leaders engineer from the top down, this book starts from a different premise. Culture is lived, not designed. It emerges through the rhythms of interaction, the negotiation of meaning, and the coordination of action over time.

What follows offers readers new ways to see their organizations more clearly, along with practical frameworks for recognizing how the micro-dynamics of relationships, rituals, and routines shape results and connect sociological insight to everyday team leadership.

What's Ahead

This book unfolds in three movements, each examining how teams coordinate under different conditions. Inside organizations teams enact routine cultural performances. As stakes shift, teams adjust their rhythms.

The opening chapters establish the sociological perspective needed to see those patterns clearly. Chapter 2 invites readers to reconsider where culture and performance reside, arguing that they do not live in individual leaders or formal structures, but in the everyday interactions of small groups. Small groups are the engines of coordination. Culture takes shape as a negotiated order, and routines are enacted as lived performances rather than fixed procedures. These ideas are presented not as abstract theory but as practical lenses for understanding how work gets done.

Chapter 3 distinguishes between ostensive goals, the simple shared understandings of what "good work" looks like, and orienting stakes, the priorities that shape how teams enact those goals in practice. Chapter 4 introduces the four small firms at the heart of this book: an organic farm, an aerospace manufacturer, a home-health care company, and a retail florist. Together, they provide a uniquely revealing vantage point for understanding teamwork, culture, and performance across organizations of all sizes.

From there, the chapters are organized around three recurring cultural performances that shape how teams pursue shared goals. The first movement examines routine stability, the everyday rhythms that allow work to proceed during periods of relative calm. Chapters 5–8 illustrate how each organization establishes reliability through shared meanings, informal authority, and negotiated expectations, even as friction and resistance remain ever present. Together, they show that stability is not the absence of conflict but the product of ongoing coordination within teams.

The second and third movements examine what happens when stable rhythms are disrupted. Routine crisis performances in Chapters 9–12 show how teams respond when something goes wrong, reputations are threatened, safety is at risk, or uncertainty escalates. In these moments, culture becomes especially visible as teams reorganize priorities, authority, and communication around their biggest fears, clarifying what must not happen and who has the power to prevent it.

Routine growth performances in Chapters 13–16 examine what unfolds when organizations pursue expansion, innovation, or legitimacy at scale. Growth, like crisis, unsettles established meanings and demands new forms of coordination, often generating tension between past identities and future ambitions. In these moments, culture becomes especially visible as teams rework priorities, authority, and identity around their growth stakes, clarifying what they hope to become and who will shape that future. These chapters show why growth efforts so often strain teams and how the redefinition of meaning ultimately determines whether expansion fragments or strengthens collective work.

This book concludes by drawing these insights together and offering guidance for leaders on how to recognize, work with, and intentionally shape their team's cultural rhythms. Chapter 17 reframes leadership not as culture-building from the top down but as learning to work with the rhythms teams already inhabit. When leaders understand how teams move between stability, crisis, and growth, friction becomes a signal rather than a failure, and flow becomes something that can be cultivated rather than commanded.

Chapter 2

The Social Life of Teams

Traditional business books tell a tidy story about performance. Leaders set strategy. Managers plan. Employees execute. Results follow.

But everyday work rarely unfolds that neatly.

Across firms, outcomes are shaped not by strategy documents but by small groups of people coordinating in real time. Deadlines are negotiated in meetings. Priorities are revised in hallway conversations. Problems are solved through informal workarounds. Frontline employees do not organize their work around mission statements or strategic objectives. They respond to immediate demands, shared expectations, and locally understood definitions of good work. Culture, authority, and meaning take shape through repeated interaction long before formal plans exert influence.

This chapter steps away from corporate abstractions and into the lived reality of work groups. It shows why strategy alone seldom guides daily activity, why culture is not installed from the top down, and how small teams become the arenas where coordination, conflict, and productivity are forged. By examining the social dynamics of everyday interaction, we can see what truly drives performance day to day.

Why Strategy Rarely Guides Everyday Work

Walk through almost any organization and ask people what they're focused on today. You'll hear about customers who need help, deadlines that are approaching, problems that just surfaced, and teammates waiting on information. What you rarely hear is anyone say is, "Today, I'm implementing strategy." Employees do not coordinate their work by referencing mission statements, strategic priorities, or five-year plans. They organize around immediate concerns, shared expectations, and locally negotiated standards of competence.

Yet business orthodoxy insists that firms should be guided by strategy. As Harvard Business School professor Michael Porter famously argued,

DOI: 10.4324/9781003779803-3

strategy is not a slogan or mission statement but a deliberate choice of activities that create unique value for customers. It forms an integrated "activity system" in which coordination, communication, and information flows align to produce results competitors cannot easily replicate.[1] In this view, strategic fit emerges from how well a firm's choices, processes, and capabilities reinforce one another.

Conceptually, the logic is straightforward. Strategy defines direction by specifying distinctive choices about how value will be created. Planning translates those choices into resource allocation and prioritized action. Strategy establishes the why and what, and planning determines the how and when.

From a distance, this model appears intuitive and orderly. It is reinforced in MBA classrooms, strategic planning templates, and executive retreats, where managers are taught to analyze markets, design strategy, allocate resources, and drive execution. The sequence looks clean, responsibilities seem defined, and authority flows predictably downward.

Up close, however, the story changes. When we move into the lived reality of everyday coordination, the tidy progression from strategy to execution begins to unravel.

Two persistent realities complicate the picture.

First, strategy rarely steers day-to-day activity. Leaders may spend months crafting strategic priorities, yet those responsible for implementation often struggle to articulate them. Managers and frontline employees organize their efforts around immediate demands and local expectations, not formal objectives. Empirical research supports what practitioners have long suspected.[2]

When this gap becomes visible, it is typically framed as a communication or alignment problem. Leaders assume strategy has not been cascaded clearly enough or reinforced consistently enough. Tools designed to bridge this divide, such as the Balanced Scorecard,[3] promise to translate broad objectives into measurable targets and keep strategy in view. Dashboards track performance and link metrics to strategic themes. Yet even with these systems in place, employees often struggle to see how their daily decisions meaningfully advance strategic intent. Enthusiasm for such tools wanes,[4] not because measurement is useless, but because clearer metrics cannot substitute for shared understanding.

Second, many organizations do not engage in formal strategy development at all. In the small companies I studied, strategic plans, formal goal systems, and performance dashboards were largely absent. There were no annual strategy binders, no formalized scorecards, and no carefully sequenced implementation roadmaps. Yet these firms still coordinated work, absorbed shocks, and, in several cases, expanded successfully.

Direction did not flow from written plans. It took shape through ongoing interaction, often uneven and sometimes contentious. Priorities were debated in meetings, recalibrated in email threads and impromptu check-ins, and occasionally ignored or openly challenged in practice. Expectations were clarified not once but repeatedly, as misunderstandings surfaced and were resolved. Collaboration was not the seamless execution of a unified plan. It was negotiated in real time and shaped by personalities, power dynamics, resource constraints, and changing circumstances. Shared understanding existed, but it was provisional and was continually reaffirmed, revised, and at times openly contested.

Taken together, these two realities challenge the conventional sequence from strategy to execution. In some organizations, strategy is articulated but fails to anchor daily coordination. In others, formal strategy barely exists at all, yet work still proceeds. In both cases, plans and performance systems tell only part of the story. Something else structures interaction, directs attention, and ultimately determines what becomes possible.

What Actually Drives the Business Engine

If strategy and planning are not what guide everyday work, what does? Across organizations, culture is the force that consistently shapes behavior through shared expectations, norms, and meanings that develop through ongoing interaction. As Peter Drucker famously argued, plans remain little more than good ideas unless a culture exists to translate them into daily practice.[5]

Much of contemporary management thinking concedes this in principle. Consultants often argue that culture must align with strategy and that a company's values, norms, and behaviors should reinforce its strategic goals. When alignment falters, strategy stalls.

Consider a hospital that adopts a strategy of patient-centered care. Leaders promote empathy, shared decision-making, and interdisciplinary collaboration. Yet in daily rounds, physicians interrupt nurses, dismiss concerns, and signal that moving quickly matters more than inviting input. No one explicitly rejects the strategy, but the everyday interaction continues to privilege hierarchy and efficiency. The initiative falters not because the vision lacks merit, but because lived norms of coordination contradict it.

Now consider a technology firm that declares innovation its top priority. Executives encourage experimentation and risk-taking. Yet in meetings, employees who present unfinished ideas are subtly dismissed, and failed projects damage reputations. No one publicly opposes innovation, but the informal rules of participation reward polish over exploration and certainty over ambiguity. Over time, employees learn that caution is safer than creativity. The strategy stalls not because innovation lacks value, but because everyday expectations redefine what competent performance requires.

Culture, then, is not merely a backdrop to performance. It is the mechanism through which coordination occurs. It shapes what people attend to, how they interpret priorities, and what actions feel appropriate or risky in the moment. Because strategy is enacted through these everyday judgments, culture ultimately determines whether strategic intent gains traction or unravels. Many leadership frameworks recognize this connection, but they often misidentify where culture originates and how it is shaped.

The Myth of the Leader as Culture Architect

We tell a familiar story about leadership and culture. Leaders articulate values, define norms, and shape the environment so behavior aligns with strategy. Edgar Schein's influential three-layer model of artifacts, espoused values, and underlying assumptions is often invoked to give this story structure.[6] In this view, vision statements, value decks, and leadership speeches express what the organization stands for, while systems, incentives, and communication channels reinforce those commitments in daily practice. When alignment falters, the explanation is predictable. Culture is said to have drifted, and responsibility returns to the top. Leaders are faulted for failing to communicate clearly, model consistently, or enforce expectations with sufficient discipline.

This account is compelling because it concentrates responsibility squarely at the top and offers clear prescriptions for action. If performance declines, leaders must clarify values and realign incentives. Yet this logic rests on a mistaken premise. Culture is not a blueprint designed by leaders and implemented by employees. It is a social order constructed and sustained through everyday interaction.

The image of the leader as culture architect endures because it promises control, the comforting belief that high-performing teams can be engineered through the right mix of values, messaging, and incentives. Yet this perspective overestimates individual agency and underestimates the durability of social arrangements. Leadership is not irrelevant, but its role must be reframed. If culture is the medium through which coordination occurs, then leadership operates within it, not above it. Leaders are not architects standing outside the system. They are participants, constrained and enabled by the rhythms their teams have already built.

If culture is not engineered, its origins must lie closer to the ground. The locus of explanation shifts away from executive intention and toward the patterned interactions through which meaning is produced and sustained over time.

Where Culture Is Made

Culture does not reside inside individuals. It exists between them. It is enacted in practice. Leaders can revise mission statements, redesign incentives, and model preferred behaviors, but they cannot directly determine what people collectively treat as important. Employees infer what truly matters by observing how decisions unfold, who is praised or promoted, how conflict is handled, and which efforts are rewarded or ignored. These signals are filtered through personal histories and crystalize into shared interpretations within work groups.

It is within teams, through close and repeated interaction, that distinct cultural logics take shape. Sociologist Gary Alan Fine calls these locally produced systems of meaning *idiocultures*.[7] They consist of shared expectations, habits, symbols, and unwritten rules that coordinate action. Small group cultures are not isolated. They are nested within broader social environments. Organizational values and industry norms provide a backdrop for action, but teams translate that backdrop into lived practice. Meaning is not simply inherited from above; it is produced, negotiated, and sustained in interaction.

Shared experiences accumulate into collective memory. Over time, patterns stabilize into recognizable ways of working. Culture emerges through interaction, lives in practice, and is reproduced through repetition. It is not installed. It is performed. Across settings of all kinds, from households and pickleball courts to start-ups and parent teacher organization meetings, groups construct local ways of operating within broader cultural frameworks.

If culture is constructed between people, we must ask how those interactions are structured and sustained.

The Interaction Order

To understand how this happens, we turn to what sociologist Erving Goffman calls the *interaction order*.[8] This term refers to the unwritten rules that govern behavior in one another's presence. Beneath formal roles and policies, these rules organize conduct in real time. They shape how people speak, interrupt, defer, joke, criticize, apologize, and assert authority.

Because the interaction order is unwritten, it is learned through participation. People absorb it by watching how meetings unfold, how disagreement is expressed, and how status is signaled. These patterns travel across settings, from shop floors to Zoom calls to hallway conversations. The interaction order functions as a form of social infrastructure, shaping behavior long before formal rules are invoked.

This perspective shifts attention away from personality and toward situated social processes. Instead of asking whether a leader is empathetic or a team member is difficult, we ask: What interactional expectations are in play? What counts as a legitimate interruption? When is silence respectful, and when is it defiance? Whose dignity must be protected? From this vantage point, culture is enacted moment by moment through these patterned exchanges.

When the interaction order operates smoothly, it is nearly invisible. When it breaks down, it becomes unmistakable. People follow its rules not because they are instructed to, but because violating them feels awkward, risky, or socially costly.

Interaction provides the structure of coordination. Performance makes that structure visible.

Performativity and Informal Scripts

Closely tied to the interaction order is what Goffman described as dramaturgical structure. Organizational life is not merely interactive. It is performative.[9] In work groups, people perform competence, professionalism, leadership, and belonging before an audience of peers. These performances are shaped less by job descriptions than by locally developed expectations about what counts as effective action.

Over time, teams develop shared understandings about what counts as good work, appropriate behavior, or stepping out of line. These expectations function as informal *scripts* that guide how members present ideas, manage disagreement, signal commitment, and interpret one another's behavior. People quickly learn what truly matters by observing who advances, whose mistakes are forgiven, and whose contributions are valued. They adjust their performances accordingly.

The interaction order and these informal scripts are powerful precisely because they feel natural. Once internalized, they guide behavior more reliably than any formal policy since violating them carries social consequences. What feels like common sense is the product of repeated, socially reinforced performance.

The Negotiated Order: Durability and Malleability of Culture

These patterns endure because they are collective. Shared meanings reduce uncertainty and create predictability. Even inefficient or frustrating cultures persist because they tell people how to behave and what to expect. New members learn "how things are done" not primarily through manuals but through observation, correction, and subtle feedback. Culture endures because it is embedded in shared understanding rather than individual preference.

These scripts and performances may appear settled, but they are never fully fixed. Up close, culture is always in motion. Teams are living social systems, not static organizational artifacts. Meanings, priorities, and interpretations are continually negotiated in everyday exchanges. Through glances, jokes, hesitations, corrections, and compromises, expectations about authority, decision-making, and acceptable conduct are subtly reinforced or revised.

A raised eyebrow during a presentation, a delayed response to an email, or a pointed follow-up question in a meeting can subtly signal what is tolerated and what is not. Imagine a team meeting where one member, Sophie, rolls her eyes at the end of her colleague's Steve's proposal. The gesture itself does not alter the culture. What matters is what follows. If others later whisper, "Did you see that?" and treat Sophie's reaction as justified, Steve's authority may be subtly weakened. If they dismiss Sophie's gesture as inappropriate, she risks marginalization instead. In these small moments of interpretation, the boundaries of influence and dissent are recalibrated. Over time, such episodes accumulate into patterns that feel stable, even as they remain open to challenge. Team culture, then, is not simply performed. It is continually *negotiated*.[10]

Negotiation here does not mean formal bargaining. It is often implicit and routine. Team members negotiate by stepping in to help or choosing not to, by speaking up or remaining silent, by enforcing a norm or letting it slide. Over time, these micro-decisions can nudge expectations, gradually reshaping what successful work looks like in practice.

Cultural change therefore unfolds slowly and unevenly through everyday interactions. It occurs as patterns of engagement evolve. Each meeting, performance review, and informal conversation reinforces or subtly adjusts the group's rules. Only when new behaviors are enacted consistently and recognized as legitimate over time can we say that culture has shifted.

Consider a new hire joining a team. Through observation and subtle feedback, the new member, Joan, quickly learns the group's unwritten scripts about meetings, authority, and standards for success. Socialization, however, is not one way. As newcomers adapt to existing norms, they also introduce alternative repertoires that can, over time, reshape culture, and alter the group's trajectory.

On Joan's team, meetings typically involve presenting fully formed recommendations. Instead of conforming, Joan offers rough, emerging ideas to invite discussion. Initially, the move feels out of place, and she may even be corrected. But Joan's prior experience at a highly innovative firm lends credibility. Over time, teammates reinterpret the deviation, thinking, "Maybe she's not unprepared. Maybe she's just thinking out loud. I know it's not how we usually talk through proposals, but it seemed to work at her last company." Soon, real-time brainstorming becomes normalized. No policy changed. No leader mandated new behavior. The interaction order shifts because the group collectively renegotiates what competent performance looks like.

Joan's influence illustrates a broader point. Stability is not the absence of negotiation but its temporary settlement. What feels natural is simply what has been repeatedly performed and affirmed. When conditions shift through crisis or growth, the negotiated order resurfaces as teams revisit assumptions, redistribute authority, and recalibrate expectations. Team cultures are durable without being fixed, flexible without being chaotic, and powerful without ever being formally designed.

If culture is negotiated in interaction, what role remains for strategy?

Rethinking the Role of Strategy

Recognizing culture as interactional and negotiated does not diminish the importance of strategy. Organizations still face competitive pressures, resource constraints, and long-term choices that require deliberate direction. Markets must be assessed. Trade-offs must be made. Investments must be prioritized. Strategic thinking remains essential.

What changes is where strategy becomes consequential.

A plan, no matter how sophisticated, does not act on its own. It enters an organization as something to be interpreted, weighed, and translated into practice. Its fate depends on how teams talk about it, whether it aligns with existing norms, and how it is incorporated into everyday routines. By the time strategy reaches the front lines, it has already been filtered through interaction and reshaped in practice.

In this sense, strategy is not a substitute for culture, nor is culture a decorative layer added to strategy. Culture is the medium through which strategy acquires force. Interactional norms determine whose voices carry weight. Informal expectations shape what counts as competent execution. Negotiated meanings determine whether change is embraced, resisted, or gradually reshaped in practice.

Strategy succeeds not when it is perfectly designed, but when it becomes embedded in the rhythms of coordination that teams already inhabit.

Notes

1 Porter, Michael E. "What Is Strategy?" *Harvard Business Review* 74, no. 6 (November–December 1996): 61–78.

2 Collis, David J., and Michael G. Rukstad. "Can You Say What Your Strategy Is?" *Harvard Business Review* 86, no. 4 (2008): 82–90.

3 Kaplan, Robert S., and David P. Norton. *The Balanced Scorecard: Translating Strategy into Action*. Boston: Harvard Business School Press, 1996.
4 Tawse, Anthony, and Pantea Tabesh. "Thirty Years with the Balanced Scorecard: What We Have Learned." *Business Horizons* 66, no. 1 (2023): 123–132.
5 Drucker, Peter F. *Management: Tasks, Responsibilities, Practices*. 1974. Reprint, New York: HarperBusiness, 2012.
6 Schein, Edgar H. *Organizational Culture and Leadership*. 4th ed. San Francisco: Jossey-Bass, 2010.
7 Fine, Gary Alan. "Small Groups and Culture Creation: The Idioculture of Little League Baseball Teams." *American Sociological Review* 44, no. 5 (1979): 733–745.
8 Goffman, Erving. "The Interaction Order: American Sociological Association, 1982 Presidential Address." *American Sociological Review* 48, no. 1 (1983): 1–17.
9 Goffman, Erving. *The Presentation of Self in Everyday Life*. 1959. Reprint, New York: Anchor Books, 2002.
10 Fine, Gary Alan. "Negotiated Orders and Organizational Cultures." *Annual Review of Sociology* 10 (1984): 239–262.

Chapter 3

When Goals Become Performances

So far, I've focused on how culture lives inside small teams, shaping how people interact, coordinate, and make sense of their work. But culture alone does not explain how work gets done. Every organization runs on routines, from hiring and onboarding to recurring meetings, production processes, and customer engagement. These activities may appear orderly from the outside, but within teams they are continually interpreted, adjusted, and negotiated. What matters is not whether teams follow routines, but how those routines are enacted in practice. Organizations do not operate on flowcharts alone. They are shaped by the way people interpret, adapt, and perform those plans together.

To understand this process, we must examine the gap between what organizations intend and what people actually do. What begins as a plan at the top is reshaped through interaction on the ground, where routines take form, meanings settle, and coordination either strengthens or frays. Policies turn into conversations. Strategic plans are translated into daily practice. This chapter traces that transformation, explaining how formal goals become the everyday cultural performances that animate them.

Ostensive Goals and Performative Routines

Organizational scholars Martha Feldman and Brian Pentland distinguish between two dimensions of any routine: the ostensive and the performative.[1,2] The ostensive dimension is the abstract template, the generalized idea of how a routine should function. The performative dimension is how people enact it in practice. The ostensive provides a reference point, and the performative gives it expression.

Consider a weekly team meeting. Teams share a basic understanding of what it is for, reviewing progress and aligning next steps. That shared understanding is the ostensive dimension. Yet the tone, participation, and decisions shift depending on deadlines, personalities, prior experiences, and emerging issues. Those situated enactments are the performative dimension.

DOI: 10.4324/9781003779803-4

This framework helps explain why routines are both stable and flexible at the same time. People draw on shared understandings of how work is supposed to unfold, and they adapt those understandings in real time as conditions change. Routines persist not because they are mechanically followed, but because actors continually reinterpret and reenact them in practice.

Building on Feldman and Pentland's insights, I retain their language but shift its level of application. Rather than focusing on the ostensive dimension of specific routines, I extend the concept to the level of organizational goals. In other words, just as routines have ostensive and performative dimensions, so too does an organization's shared understanding of what it is trying to accomplish. Across teams, people develop a simplified, collective sense of what good work looks like and what they are trying to accomplish together. This shared frame does not originate in strategy documents or mission statements. It emerges through experience and guides everyday decisions, shaping how routines are interpreted, enacted, and revised in practice.

I call these shared orientations *ostensive goals*. Ostensive goals are the simplified, shared understandings of what good work looks like that guide everyday judgment across a team.

Unlike strategies or formal objectives, ostensive goals are not detailed plans. They are shared conceptions of successful performance that anchor coordination across routines. Because they are clear and portable, they carry across everyday work and moments of disruptions, providing continuity even as specific routines evolve.

Wherever people coordinate over time, they gravitate toward simplified, shared definitions of what good work looks like. These goals are often surprisingly mundane, such as making great pastries in a bakery, creating an intuitive program for a software company, generating reliable returns in a financial firm, and helping patients achieve healthy outcomes in a physician's office. Their power lies in their simplicity. Precisely because they are clear and widely understood, they become shared reference points for evaluating action and settling disagreement.

Ostensive goals set the destination while leaving teams to determine the route. They offer no instructions for timing, coordination, interpersonal dynamics, or decision-making. On their own, they provide orientation, not action. Only through everyday interaction do people translate these abstract ideas into concrete routines.

Variation emerges in *performance*. Enactments depend on employees' skills, habits, experiences, interpretations, and relationships, as well as on local team dynamics and organizational conditions. Two teams may share the same ostensive goal—such as delivering excellent care, producing high-quality products, or serving customers well—yet enact it differently.

People observe one another, adjust to unfolding situations, negotiate responsibilities, and coordinate in real time. Rather than following a single script, teams draw from a repertoire of possibilities, continually reconstructing routines as circumstances change.

Together, the ostensive and performative dimensions of routines anchor this book's framework. Every organization operates around a small set of ostensive goals that give people a shared sense of what success looks like in practice. Leaders do not always articulate these goals directly. Modern management often favors strategies that sound complex and differentiated over goals that are simple and concrete. Yet beneath mission statements, strategy decks, performance dashboards, and consulting jargon, a basic understanding of what truly matters inevitably emerges.

Employees are rarely confused by the clutter for long. Through everyday conversations, observations, and experiences, they learn what is valued and rewarded, what mistakes carry consequences, and what quality work really means. Over time, these shared interpretations solidify into the team's practical definition of success and anchor everyday performances.

Ostensive goals provide direction. Routines organize that direction into patterns of work. Performances reveal how those patterns are enacted, adapted, and sustained as conditions change.

When the Stakes Shift, So Does Performance

Shared direction points teams toward a goal, but it does not show them how to move together in real time. The same organizational goal can produce calm routines one day, intense collaboration the next, and disruption the week after. No organization operates in a stable environment. Markets fluctuate, crises erupt, workflows break down, and new opportunities arise. As circumstances evolve, teams must continually recalibrate how they work by reorganizing resources, renegotiating roles, and adjusting expectations to pursue the same underlying goals amid changing conditions.

Again and again, I saw teams hold fast to their ostensive goals even as circumstances shifted dramatically. What changed was the sense of what was at stake in pursuing them. I use the term *orienting stakes* to describe the underlying threats or opportunities that heighten the consequences of action and reorganize how work is performed.

These shifts do not occur because leaders redesign culture from above. They emerge within small groups, where adaptation becomes possible. It is within teams that people draw on shared histories, norms, and emotional understandings to answer the practical questions that matter every day: How urgent is this? Who should step in? When should we change course? Small group cultures supply the repertoire of responses that create resilience and allow organizations to move fluidly as pressures shift.

Across every organization I studied, culture did not operate as a single, stable force. Instead, teams moved through a small set of recurring performance modes that shaped how work was accomplished. These shifts were driven not by formal strategy or policy but by changing stakes, shared expectations, and the emotional cadence of daily work. Three core cultural performances, or rhythms, structure how teams responded to changing conditions.

Routine stability performances anchor everyday operations through reliable habits, clear roles, and familiar routines that keep work predictable and efficient.

Routine crisis performances reorganize work when something goes wrong, tightening coordination, shifting authority, and resetting priorities to restore order.

Routine growth performances stretch teams toward new possibilities, disrupting established patterns of work as organizations pursue innovation, expansion, or new markets.

Although each performance is activated by shifting orienting stakes, they differ in temporal focus and emotional intensity. Routine stability sustains the present, allowing teams to rely on familiar patterns and shared expectations. Routine crisis narrows attention around preventing immediate loss, tightening authority and accelerating decision-making. Routine growth redirects attention toward an imagined future, stretching routines as teams pursue what the organization might become.

Orienting stakes explain why the same team, pursuing the same ostensive goal, may centralize authority in one moment and invite collaboration in another, move cautiously in one context and take bold risks in the next. Stakes reshape how priorities are interpreted, how relationships are navigated, and how resources are mobilized. In doing so, they determine how shared goals are enacted.

Stability functions as the cultural baseline to which teams continually return. When no urgent threat or compelling opportunity dominates attention, coordination feels coherent and competent. Crisis and growth mark departures from that equilibrium. Teams shift into these modes as circumstances change and move back toward stability as stakes recede. Organizational resilience lies not in remaining stable but in moving among these performances without losing clarity about the ostensive goal that anchors them.

These performances are not fixed scripts but evolving patterns. They shift as team histories deepen, relationships change, and emotions rise or settle. Leaders must therefore act less like engineers designing static systems and more like DJs reading the room, sensing shifts in tempo, and guiding coordination as the rhythm of work changes. The ostensive goal remains constant. What shifts are the orienting stakes that shape how that goal is enacted in any given moment.

The chapters that follow bring these rhythms to life. Drawing on detailed examples from the four firms where I conducted fieldwork, they show how the plans, goals, and routines that appear orderly from a distance are continually reshaped through interaction. As orienting stakes shift, teams do not abandon their goals. They perform them differently, reorganizing coordination, authority, and meaning in real time. What begins as an abstract idea of what the organization is trying to achieve becomes, through daily action, a set of lived performances. Together, these hidden rhythms explain how work really gets done.

Notes

1 Feldman, Martha S., and Brian T. Pentland. "Reconceptualizing Organizational Routines as a Source of Flexibility and Change." *Administrative Science Quarterly* 48, no. 1 (2003): 94–118.
2 Pentland, Brian T., and Martha S. Feldman. "Organizational Routines as a Unit of Analysis." *Industrial and Corporate Change* 14, no. 5 (2005): 793–815.

Chapter 4

Landing Gear, Lettuce, Bouquets, and Home Health Aides

At 7 a.m., a farm owner stands knee-deep in mud, harvesting greens before the heat settles in. Across the river, a bell rings in a small manufacturing plant, echoing across concrete floors and steel machines. A few towns away, a home health care scheduler scrolls through her phone, scrambling to fill a last-minute cancellation before a client wakes up alone. Two hours north, in the back room of a florist shop, siblings argue again about who forgot to place the Mother's Day balloon order.

None of these moments appear on strategy decks. No mission statement explains how to respond when a volunteer arrives unmotivated, a machinist runs late, a caregiver calls out sick a caregiver calls out sick, or a sibling forgets a critical order. Yet these are the moments when work comes alive. They are where plans meet reality and where teams reveal who they are.

In small organizations, there is little room to hide. Decisions travel quickly. Mistakes are visible. Relationships matter immediately. When someone hesitates, improvises, or pushes back, everyone feels it. The workday develops a rhythm shaped less by formal roles than by who steps in, who waits, who speaks up, and who absorbs the strain.

From the outside, these businesses may appear informal or under-resourced. From the inside, they are tightly coordinated systems sustained by shared expectations and constant adjustment. Team members learn, often without realizing it, how meetings unfold, which shortcuts are tolerated, when disagreement is welcome, and when it carries risk.

Small businesses offer rare access to the texture of everyday work. Owners and managers are often more willing to grant sustained entry, making it possible to observe not just what people say about their work, but what they do on shop floors, how they schedule clients, how they experience pressures during peak seasons, and how they handle crises. Their size also makes coordination visible. By embedding myself in these firms and working alongside their teams, I saw how culture is enacted, how coordination is negotiated, and how rhythm emerged from people working together over

DOI: 10.4324/9781003779803-5

time. There are few buffers and formal layers, and little distance between decisions and consequences.

This chapter outlines the research process and presents the four organizations that ground the book's analysis. Rolling Hills, AeroGears, ElderCare, and Thorny Rose serve as its central cases. Though they span agriculture, manufacturing, home health care, and retail services, they share a common feature: each reveals how interaction orders shape team culture on the ground.

From Observer to Teammate

Gaining access to these organizations required persistence, personal networks, and a willingness to take on real work. I approached each not as an outside expert or consultant but as someone prepared to contribute labor in exchange for entry. Sometimes, that meant responding to an immediate staffing need. Other times, it involved conversations with owners and managers willing to take a risk on letting a researcher inside their business. What ultimately opened doors was not my credentials but my readiness to show up, follow directions, and be useful within the everyday flow of work.

In exchange for access, I committed to protecting the anonymity of the people and organizations who allowed me into their working lives. I use pseudonyms for all individuals and companies, and I have altered identifying details, such as locations, timelines, or organizational specifics, without changing the underlying social dynamics being analyzed. These choices follow standard ethnographic practice, where confidentiality ensures that participants speak and act naturally, preserving fidelity to the social processes that matter. In this respect, the approach resembles journalism, where sources are protected so that experiences, tensions, and contradictions can be described honestly.

Once inside, access deepened through participation rather than formal permission. Someone might call me "professor" or joke during tense moments, asking, "I wonder what the management doc thinks about this." But any special treatment that might have followed from that acknowledgment never materialized. I was scheduled, trained, corrected, and relied upon like any other employee.

During my first week at AeroGears, I was reprimanded for arriving five minutes late and told that a severe morning thunderstorm and multiple car wrecks on my commute were not valid excuses for tardiness. At Thorny Rose, after more than ten hours of physical labor, I briefly took a phone call from my fiancé while still working. Less than two minutes in, I was told, "You're not getting paid to be on the phone."

Although everyone knew I was there to study teamwork, credibility was earned the same way as every other team member—through reliability, shared effort, and endurance during unglamorous moments.

Studying Work from the Inside

Across the four firms, I spent roughly eighteen months embedded as an employee, typically working one to two days per week at each business. This rotating schedule allowed me to observe variations in work rhythms, staffing patterns, and weekly routines. I also aligned my time with critical organizational moments, such as AeroGears' AS9100 accreditation process and the Valentine's Day production rush at Thorny Rose, when coordination demands intensified and cultural dynamics became especially visible.

My primary data came from daily field notes written during and immediately after work. Because much of my work at ElderCare, AeroGears, and Thorny Rose was computer-based, I was often able to write notes in near real time as events unfolded, documenting interactions, capturing detailed descriptions, and recording conversations verbatim. When on-site notetaking was not possible, I relied on brief written jottings in a pocket notebook and voice memos recorded during commutes, which I expanded into full field notes each evening. I supplemented these observations with informal conversations, repeated formal interviews with owners, managers, and employees, as well as internal documents, emails, and industry publications. Together, these sources provided a grounded view of how teams actually function day to day.

When Belonging Becomes Automatic

Over time, I became embedded in each organization's team, performing its cultural practices alongside other members. These routines did not simply become visible; they became embodied. I internalized the team's unwritten norms, becoming most aware of them when I inadvertently crossed their boundaries.

For example, while sitting at my desk at AeroGears, I let out a small but audible fart. In most workplaces, this would be inappropriate. At Thorny Rose, however, bodily sounds and smells were a source of humor. The siblings at the florist, especially the brothers, regularly passed gas and joked about it. As I became more comfortable and gained acceptance within the group, I occasionally joined in.

At AeroGears, that kind of behavior ran counter to the team's norms. After passing gas, I instinctively started to laugh, then looked up from my computer and realized I was not among the Thorny Rose team. There was no joking or bonding around such moments. I covered my smile and returned to work, hoping others might attribute the sound to a squeaky drawer nearby, however unlikely. Experiences like this revealed how deeply team-specific scripts shape behavior, often beneath conscious awareness.

Such moments were rarely consequential, yet they underscored a central argument of this book, namely that belonging is learned through social, collaborative practice. Team cultures are not abstract values. They are embodied patterns of action that shape what feels normal, acceptable, or risky in a given setting.

The Context, the Teams, and the Work: The Firms Behind the Patterns

Rolling Hills

Rolling Hills is a ten-year-old, sixty-acre organic farm organized around a weekly on-site Community Supported Agriculture (CSA) program, supplemented by restaurant sales, and a weekend farmers market. CSA members pick up produce during the growing season. Lower-grade crops, along with grocery store purchases, feed farmhands or are preserved for winter. The farm also produces eggs and keeps dairy cows. Daily operations depend heavily on rotating volunteers who trade labor for food and housing, making coordination and consistency an ongoing challenge.

The Operating Environment

Rolling Hills sits amid a landscape of working farms, about ninety minutes from a nearby city. A long gravel driveway leads to a farmhouse where volunteers stayed. A converted garage serves as the CSA distribution area, with refrigeration, storage, and a small certified organic kitchen added during my time there. The kitchen inside the home functioned as the social and coordination hub. Meals, small talk, and informal planning unfolded there, alongside subtle moments of correction and conflict avoidance. Beyond the house stretched fields, greenhouses, goat pens, compost piles, roaming chickens, and two cows.

Leadership and Authority

The farm's founder, Penelope, framed Rolling Hills as both a personal dream and a community project. Guided by Rudolf Steiner's philosophy of biodynamic farming, she treated the farm as a closed system where food scraps fed animals, manure became mulch, and mulch sustained future crops. As she often put it, "the world is a good and beautiful place" that can "naturally provide" what is needed. She worked with relentless energy, moving constantly between harvesting, cooking, canning, organizing, and teaching. Volunteers described her as nurturing but demanding.

Her husband, Ross, managed bookkeeping but rarely worked in the fields. Filipe, an immigrant from Costa Rica, was the only full-time paid employee. Exceptionally fast and strong, he also brought an unpredictable humor. On my first day, Penelope warned me that he asked personal questions that sometimes veered into inappropriateness. Within five minutes of meeting him, he put that warning to the test. "How many girlfriends do you have?" he asked. "Just one," I replied. He looked stunned. "One?! Why only one." I chose not to respond.

He often joked loudly, mimicked animals, and laughed at his own comments. He reminisced about a previous job where he worked long hours but always had Sundays off, calling it "a good life."

Aiko, a long-term volunteer and aspiring farmer, embodied the farm's ethos. She became Penelope's most trusted helper and my primary informant. Tireless and steady, she assumed responsibilities others avoided. After leaving Rolling Hills, she moved to a larger farm to continue her training.

Around these core figures, a shifting group of five to ten volunteers participated at any given time, bringing different motivations and levels of experience. The farm's team rhythm was therefore fragile, often dependent on a few reliable people.

My Role on the Team

I worked primarily on CSA preparation, harvesting crops, setting up weekly distributions, and preparing produce for restaurant orders. I also assisted with pricing, cooking, cleaning, and special events such as farm dinners. During peak seasons, I worked two days a week and stayed overnight. In slower months, I reduced my time to one day per week. I collected data across two full CSA seasons.

AeroGears

AeroGears is a nearly forty-year-old aerospace and commercial manufacturing firm. The company has shifted from primarily local commercial work to national contracts, including gun manufacturers and, more recently, government contracts producing parts for military aircraft. These contracts became possible after AeroGears earned AS9100 accreditation, the aerospace industry's quality management standard.

While the firm continues to produce a wide range of commercial components, including elevator parts and Geiger counter pieces, the move into aerospace raised expectations around precision, documentation, and coordination. Aerospace parts required higher-grade materials and tighter tolerances.

Regardless of client, work followed blueprints specifying exact measurements and allowable variance. Jobs ranged from small batches to runs of hundreds. Machinists monitored tolerances throughout production, while quality control inspected select pieces from each batch. For long-time commercial clients, employees sometimes exercised judgment when parts drifted slightly outside specification, relying on experience to assess functional viability. Aerospace contracts allowed no such discretion.

Daily time at AeroGears was structured by a bell. The workday began at 7 a.m., with additional bells marking break, lunch, and closing time. Alex, the quality control manager, viewed the bell as unnecessary. "You don't think they can read the big clock on that wall out there?" he asked. Most employees worked Saturdays and logged about fifty-four hours per week, including what workers called "forced overtime."

The Operating Environment

AeroGears operated in a large two-floor red-brick building that the company moved into eight years before I arrived, leaving what one long-term employee described as "an old falling apart building in the middle of a busy street." The shop floor housed expensive computerized cutting machines, many running nearly around the clock.

The first floor housed the machinery, a break room, and the floor manager's office, which sat behind a glass wall overlooking production. Upstairs, a main office also overlooked the factory floor and contained desks for all non-machinists, including Leo, Colleen, Alex, and me, as well as a conference room. Leo, the owner, also maintained a private office in addition to his desk in the shared workspace. He rarely used it, often jokingly referring to it as his "executive suite." From my desk in the main office, I regularly overheard and participated in management conversations about delays, staffing, quality concerns, and client relationships.

Leadership and Authority

Authority centered on a small leadership core. Jack, the floor manager, held the most power after Leo. Nearly all floor employees reported to Jack. Alex, my immediate supervisor, was third in the firm's hierarchy of responsibility and influence. A former union secretary with experience in larger manufacturing firms, he held strong views about resource allocation and the treatment of employees. He processed incoming orders, assembled materials and documents, and organized jobs before releasing them to the floor. Colleen, the factory secretary, managed billing, invoices, and payroll.

Leo was brisk and energetic, in his early fifties, and served as the company's primary salesperson. A consultant who introduced me to him remarked that Leo "certainly has the gift of gab." Alex agreed. Leo "is a great salesman" who can "talk down clients that were pissed at us...and by the end of the conversation they're laughing."

Jack enforced punctuality and discipline on the floor. Though he would regularly joke with staff, most machinists disliked his sharp judgments and frequent criticism. Despite his intense work ethic, most employees felt his leadership limited the company's growth.

Alex worked hard, teased others constantly, and resisted letting work spill into his personal life. After a tense exchange about a delayed order, he simply shrugged and replied, "On Saturday it's going to be beautiful. Because that's where my head is. Is it 5 o'clock yet? I need to get home and watch the Yankees. Ya know, I don't get paid enough to pull my hair out about these things." Even his desk calendar reflected this boundary, listing television shows and weekend activities like "Deer Hunting," but no meetings or production targets.

Colleen functioned as social glue. She joked constantly with managers and customers, often answering the phone with, "Yes, my daaaarling." or "Hello, dear." Leo said she had "a way with people that puts them in a good mood." Her loud laugh regularly filled the office.

Beyond the management team, AeroGears employed roughly twenty-two workers organized by skill and seniority: machinists, deburring specialists, quality control staff, programmers, and administrative support. Many had worked there for over a decade, including European immigrants trained through apprenticeship systems. Turnover among newer hires, however, was high, posing an ongoing challenge for a firm trying to grow.

My Role on the Team

I initially worked two days per week, later reducing to one. Before I started, Leo had only a vague idea of what I would do. On my first day, Alex told me Leo assumed I would help install new planning and scheduling software because I was "a bright, self-starter." The software was never adopted, something Alex predicted early on. Instead, my work centered on quality systems, including reviewing blueprints, updating protocols, and assisting with internal audits to maintain AS9100 standards.

ElderCare

ElderCare is a franchised home health care company that places aides in the homes of elderly clients requiring varying levels of assistance. This location served a largely upper–middle-class suburban county and was in its second year of operation when I arrived. ElderCare was looking to expand rapidly during the time I worked there. The company added dozens of aides, new administrative staff, and additional service lines. The company began serving disabled children, supporting nursing homes, and coordinating hospital-to-home transitions. Growth fueled opportunity but also strained coordination, as roles and routines were still taking shape.

The Operating Environment

ElderCare operated out of a nondescript, two-story office building on a busy suburban street. The office was arranged in a simple square layout, with a short hallway leading to my desk beside a large receptionist station and two other workspaces. A dry-erase board hung nearby, usually blank. A doored office sat in the corner, modest and orderly, with a small lamp casting a warm glow across the desk. Behind the main work area was a narrow room with filing cabinets, a printer, a coffee station, and a small conference room used interchangeably for meetings, interviews, and lunch breaks.

Leadership and Authority

The business was owned by Alice, an ambitious former executive manager who long wanted to run her own company. After being laid off from her corporate job, she decided to "finally go for it." She chose franchising after researching success rates, noting that franchise owners tended to fare better than independent start-ups. Her interest in home health care was personal. She had been frustrated by the care her father received and believed too few providers offered genuinely compassionate service.

Alice was a confident, no-nonsense leader who dressed in polished corporate attire, although her pink, sparkly phone case hinted at a playful side. Employees described her as an "excellent communicator and an attentive listener." She stayed involved in nearly every aspect of the business, often fielding questions ranging from scheduling problems to computer glitches. At times, she responded to office staff with, "That's why you're here, to figure that out," but she did so gently, and employees respected her decisiveness. A consultant who worked with her periodically described her as "a smart business woman…able to take the risk of getting this business going in a difficult industry."

Jenn, the office administrator, functioned as ElderCare's logistical and emotional hub. She was responsible for scheduling, billing, payroll, and daily operations. Friendly, energetic, and quick to empathize, she joked easily with aides and clients. One elderly client she called "my boyfriend" phoned regularly just to talk. When a nurse spoke with him during Jenn's lunch break, she teased, "My boyfriend's cheating on me?!"

Jenn was also adept at managing tension. She frequently persuaded caregivers to take last-minute shifts, saying, "Can you do a favor for me, my love," followed by "I owe you one." After hanging up, she might mutter, "That was a lot of fun, kissing her ass." Beyond office duties, Jenn drove aides to job sites, handled after-hours emergencies, and often took work home. Though she sometimes complained about added responsibilities, she ultimately viewed Alice as a good boss, laughing that "you've got to be crazy to open a business like this." Jenn remained with ElderCare for most of my fieldwork, eventually leaving for a job that allowed her to work from home.

ElderCare began with roughly thirty "available aides," about half of whom had scheduled shifts at any given time. Most worked for multiple agencies, accepting assignments from whichever firm contacted them first. The majority were immigrants. Some placements involved caring for couples or serving as live-in aides, arrangements that were more lucrative for both the company and the workers.

Finally, two part-time nurses regularly visited the office to complete paperwork and provide Alice with client and aide updates, although they primarily assessed clients, developed care plans, and monitored aides' performance in clients' homes.

My Role on the Team

I was brought in to assist with Joint Commission on Accreditation of Healthcare Organizations (JCAHO), a quality management certification more commonly associated with hospitals. Franchise headquarters required this for market differentiation. Like AeroGears' AS9100 process, JCAHO required extensive documentation, new standard operation procedures, and consistent performance. After certification was secured, I helped organize employee and client files, built tracking spreadsheets for aide credentials, assisted with sales efforts, and represented the office at the annual franchisee conference, where I met administrators, nurses, and owners from across the system.

Thorny Rose

Thorny Rose is a third-generation, family-owned florist run by four siblings who all function as managers. The business blends retail and wholesale revenues, with most income coming from retail sales: everyday arrangements, funeral and gravesite work, and major holiday spikes on Valentine's Day and Mother's Day. Seasonal offerings add to the mix, from Christmas trees and gift baskets in winter to vegetables from a small garden in summer, alongside year-round décor sales. During the time I worked, the shop increasingly focused on expanding their wedding business.

On the wholesale side, Thorny Rose supplies trees to other florists, plants to gravesites, and religious items to churches. Long-standing community ties place the business at the center of local civic life.

The Operating Environment

Thorny Rose sits at the end of a small strip mall on a busy suburban road. Alongside the shop is a fenced garden center that, Nicholas, one of the brothers, envisioned as a "Home Depot-style area with plants, pots, and gardening equipment." In practice, it functioned as a seasonal staging ground: plants in spring, a refrigerator trailer for Valentine's Day, and a full Christmas tree sales operation in winter. Nine months into my fieldwork, Nicholas added a small garden plot for tomatoes and peppers.

A long greenhouse between the lot and the store housed empty pots and struggling plants "being nursed back to life." Inside, the shop felt perpetually crowded and improvised. Plants filled every corner, ribbon spools were scattered across tables, buckets of flowers were set out to "bloom," and worktables were constantly in use. At the front sat a consultation area for weddings and funerals, sometimes surrounded by memorial displays. On at least two occasions, I watched Lilia move a stand reading "In Loving Memory" to make room for wedding clients.

Behind the register was the administrative back area, cluttered with aging equipment and shelves packed with paperwork. Julian, the oldest sibling, insisted he had "a system." After I reorganized a stack of papers and he struggled to locate a customer order he remembered placing under a keyboard, I never attempted to declutter again.

The basement refrigerator opened behind a heavy wooden door into a dark, damp room packed with flowers awaiting processing. Nearby tables supported wedding production. In the sub-basement, small rooms stored supplies and years of records in cardboard rose boxes. Julian shrugged at the disorder: "You must think I'm crazy, but this is how we do it."

Leadership and Authority

The sibling management team was intense and tightly intertwined. Ranging from early thirties to late forties, they were physically imposing enough that a family friend described them as "hulking."

Julian was the steady center, widely regarded as "the head" of both the family and the business. He carried the heaviest administrative burden, managing bills, taxes, invoicing, and insurance while also handling floral production and phone orders. Friendly with customers and quick moving despite chronic back pain, he described his devotion to the shop as a sacrifice: "This is what the business requires." He framed his commitment to "continue the family business legacy."

Lilia was the most polished and customer-oriented sibling, focusing primarily on weddings. She reduced her hours not long after I started working because she said she could not tolerate constant conflict. Her care for customers could be striking. When a woman came to buy flowers for her son's grave, Lilia added a corsage at no cost and told her, "This is for you to look especially beautiful when visiting your son."

Tyler, the youngest sibling, played the role of jokester and chief source of gossip but she was also the least experienced. She often sought approval rather than feedback and favored "the most beautiful pink and purple flowers," sometimes using the best blooms without considering downstream needs. When floral designs looked particularly vibrant, Lilia would ask, "Was Tyler making arrangements this morning?" Nicholas replied, "Yeah, why? They look good." Lilia would respond, "I figured. All the purple flowers are gone." Tyler lived nearby and periodically "disappeared" during the day, returning with homecooked food. Though technically responsible for some hourly staff, she often behaved more like an employee than a manager.

Nicholas ran much of the daily operations and possessed the strongest personality and the hardest edge. He barked orders and closely monitored productivity. Hearing laughter from an employee in the basement, Nicholas once snapped, "Why is he laughing?!" When Julian replied, "Uhh, maybe someone told a joke. What's wrong?" Nicholas responded, "If he's happy, he's not working hard enough." Employees called him "the General," and siblings joked about him as "El Diablo Blanco" a nod to their South American heritage. Even the nickname "Pops" reflected his self-appointed patriarch stance with nonfamily staff.

Yet Nicholas was also self-aware. He admitted he had good ideas but had "trouble saying it in ways that get my family on board. And then I get angry because I don't think they're listening." After certain outbursts, he would concede, "This time, I had no right to yell," sometimes apologizing before later framing his anger as necessary for efficiency.

Although Nicholas often said he could earn more elsewhere, he described his commitment as duty: "Julian and I work hard all the time here for our family and for the legacy of this place." He regularly invoked their father as a moral guide and insisted that "customers always come first." Still, his values clashed with Julian's. When Julian gave Tyler time off to see her daughter's school play, Nicholas remarked, "You know that Julian always puts family before business. Always." Julian shot back, "You always put money before family."

The shop operated seven days a week, with Julian and Nicholas working nearly nonstop during peak seasons.

My Role on the Team

I began as Julian's "assistant," handling administrative tasks the siblings avoided. I also managed online orders from the shop's website, along with orders transmitted through Teleflora and FTD that Thorny Rose fulfilled. When orders from these two online platforms arrived, they required a rapid decision: accept, reject, or negotiate price and delivery time.

The system ran on a strict thirty-minute clock. If no response was recorded, the shop was obligated to fulfill the order under the original terms. Late responses still required completion but triggered negative marks that lowered rankings and reduced future orders. Because online fulfillment was often neglected, orders sometimes slipped through the cracks. Julian and Nicholas hoped I could develop a clearer tracking system to reduce missed work when I was not present.

How Work Actually Happens

By working alongside these teams rather than observing from a distance, the patterns of everyday coordination became visible. Whether harvesting lettuce, machining aerospace parts, coordinating care work, or building floral arrangements, employees relied on shared expectations, informal rules, emotional cues, and hard-earned experience to keep work moving. Together, these four organizations offer contrasting but complementary windows into team life.

Across industries and ownership structures, they reveal how culture is enacted and coordination negotiated under shifting conditions. Each team developed its own way of determining what mattered, who led in particular moments, and how problems were handled when plans broke down. Leadership shifted with the task. Credibility was earned through effort. Belonging emerged through participation. Power did not always follow job titles, and expertise often carried more weight than formal authority.

These organizations were not smooth or harmonious, but they were functional. Their capacity to operate rested on cultural routines that guided behavior, shaped expectations, and helped members interpret uncertainty together. In these settings, culture was not something written. It was something performed.

With this context in place, the chapters that follow show how teams sustain order not by clinging to stability but by adapting how they perform their goals as circumstances change.

Movement I

Stability

Chapter 5

In Step

Routine Stability and the Comfort of Coordination

Organizations often devote enormous time and energy to crafting mission statements, values frameworks, strategic plans, and carefully calibrated objectives meant to define what quality work should look like. These artifacts promise alignment and excellence through formal design. Yet inside the firms I studied, everyday coordination rarely hinged on such blueprints. Stability rested on something more grounded: shared, practical understandings of what effective performance meant in context.

Ostensive goals, introduced in Chapter 3, provide a steady reference point for action. They anchor what teams are trying to accomplish while leaving the details of execution open to interpretation. Concise and memorable, they shape daily work more powerfully than corporate slogans ever could.

To see what I mean, recall the earlier examples of making great pastries in a bakery, creating an intuitive program for a software company, generating reliable returns in a financial firm, and helping patients achieve healthy outcomes in a physician's office. Each captures a simple, high-level understanding that anchors collective work. On their own, such ostensive goals do not specify procedures or dictate decisions. They cannot anticipate every circumstance. But they provide a starting point. From there, teams develop routines and coordination practices that translate these abstract understandings into everyday performance.

In the firms I observed, these guiding ideas were rarely written down or formally declared. They became visible through conversations, corrections, stories, and judgments about whether work was done well. Rather than being formally defined by strategy, they were enacted and reinforced through interaction. Across hundreds of hours of observation and interviews, these patterns distilled into four stabilizing reference points. They are not formal targets or mission statements but simple, shared definitions of what good work looks like:

Rolling Hills: Tasty and attractive produce
AeroGears: A precise part

DOI: 10.4324/9781003779803-7

ElderCare: Compassionate care
Thorny Rose: Beautiful arrangements

But naming the goal is only the beginning. To deliver consistently, employees must understand how that goal is interpreted within their organization, including its norms, workflows, habits, histories, and unwritten rules. Through repeated interaction, teams develop a shared sense of what the ostensive goal demands in practice.

Over time, certain interpretations settle into recognizable patterns. Members learn what counts as competent work, who holds influence in particular situations, and how problems are typically handled. These patterns are not imposed from above but emerge through ongoing interaction and gradually become taken for granted and understood as "reality," as Gary Alan Fine argues.[1,2] When the negotiated order stabilizes, it feels natural.

The first of the three recurring cultural performances is routine stability. This is the ordering of resources, relationships, and everyday practices that allows teams to accomplish ostensive goals during periods of relative calm, when there is no immediate crisis and no active push for growth. Routine stability is not necessarily the most efficient mode of operating, but it is the most familiar and comfortable. It carries a quiet confidence. Roles are clear. Expectations are predictable. Time feels expansive rather than urgent. Authority rests in settled patterns rather than active assertion.

How Order Holds

If ostensive goals define what good work looks like, routine stability performances define how that work is reliably accomplished in everyday practice. I identified each firm's routine stability performance by observing how employees directed one another, explained their work to me, and coordinated during ordinary, uneventful periods. Their taken-for-granted patterns appeared as follows:

Rolling Hills: Holistic work activities
AeroGears: Stick to your task
ElderCare: Collaborative effort
Thorny Rose: Whatever needs to get done

These routines stabilize expectations and make coordination feel natural. But stability does not eliminate friction. It manages it. Even within settled routines, tensions surface. When someone steps outside a role, fails to coordinate, or questions established expectations, conflict can emerge. In the absence of a major disruption, such frictions rarely fracture the system. Stability endures because employees reaffirm the cultural order through countless small interactions.

The next three chapters examine how routine stability operates in each firm. For clarity and comparison, I group the cases by shared themes that emerged from my observations. Chapter 6 explores Rolling Hills and AeroGears, where a parental style of leadership anchors everyday order. Chapter 7 turns to ElderCare and Thorny Rose, which operate under shared but often contentious leadership structures. Chapter 8 concludes the section with key takeaways and practical lessons for leaders seeking to build durable stability within their teams.

Notes

1 Fine, Gary Alan. "Negotiated Orders and Organizational Cultures." *Annual Review of Sociology* 10 (1984): 239–262.
2 Fine, Gary Alan. *Tiny Publics: A Theory of Group Action and Culture*. New York: Russell Sage Foundation, 2012.

Chapter 6

Authority as Care

Rolling Hills

Ostensive goal: Tasty and attractive produce
Routine stability performance: Holistic work activities

Leadership as Mothering

At Rolling Hills, routine stability centered on performing quality through holistic coordination in daily work. In practice, this meant cultivating a shared sense of responsibility for growing healthy, high-quality crops. This work was anchored in a maternal style of leadership that blurred the boundaries between care and control. Penelope often referred to the farmhands as "my children," positioning herself as both caretaker and manager.

Penelope's mornings began around 5:30 a.m. She picked up Filipe, stopped by a café that bought the farm's produce and collected day-old pastries, before returning home to make oatmeal, humming as she roused volunteers awake. By 6:30 a.m., she rang a bell and sang a constantly evolving "Good Morning" song.

Her maternal tone carried through the day. If evening gatherings grew loud, she would appear at the doorway with a firm "lower your volume." At breakfast, she might praise us for being "so quiet last night" or scold us for keeping her and Ross, her husband, awake. During dinner prep, she once turned to those of us chatting at the table and said, "If you're not helping, take your conversation to the living room," a remark that made me feel like a child being sent away so the adults could work.

Farmhands noticed this dynamic as well. One joked that she came to the farm "to get away from my mother," only to find Penelope filling much the same role.

The Appearance of Choice

Volunteers came to the farm for many reasons, including community, free room and board, or an interest in agriculture. Regardless of why they arrived,

DOI: 10.4324/9781003779803-8

most performed the necessary core farm work with little coaxing, harvesting enough produce for the weekly CSA.

Each morning at breakfast, Penelope wrote the day's tasks on a dry-erase board. The list included harvesting specific quantities of vegetables, collecting goat dung, weeding, spreading coffee grounds, and so on. She walked through the tasks and asked who wanted each job, adding names as people volunteered. After breakfast, the board was moved to the garage so everyone could track progress and take on additional work as needed.

Although this ritual resembled shared decision-making, Penelope often overruled volunteers' choices. She vetoed assignments when she did not trust someone's skill or when new volunteers lacked experience. As she told me, she "can't trust some people to do things correctly." Long-term farmhands learned that she usually had particular people in mind for certain jobs, especially right before CSA pickup. If those people didn't volunteer, she simply assigned them, gently but firmly. "Voluntold" was a term frequently used by farmhands, and few pushed back against her assignments.

We joked about the illusion of choice she worked so hard to maintain, but most of us accepted it. Experience mattered. Tasks had to get done. Contributing to the CSA felt like part of our obligation to our mother-leader.

Learning the Work Together

New farmhands were usually paired with someone experienced, even if many arrived assuming harvesting was simply "picking fruit off a tree or tugging vegetables out of the ground," as one newcomer initially thought. In practice, each crop required skill. Carrots had to be dug without snapping, kale bundled without bruising, cherry tomatoes plucked without breaking their skins, and cucumbers harvested at precisely the right moment. Experienced volunteers passed along these skills as part of the farm's informal training system.

Penelope established this structure. She preferred to teach every new volunteer herself but lacked the time, so she relied on trusted farmhands to provide hands-on instruction. She occasionally offered suggestions at breakfast, but day-to-day guidance came from volunteers helping one another. Over time, farmhands recognized that Penelope was preoccupied with tasks they rarely assisted with and that routine harvesting could be learned and completed without her direct oversight.

Framing Holistic Work

When new volunteers arrived, Penelope framed the farm as more than a workplace, emphasizing both spiritual and personal growth. I received the same brief orientation she offered others, and its themes were reinforced daily over shared meals. At breakfast and dinner, Penelope recited prayers, often drawn from Indian texts, while we discussed the flavors of the vegetables we had harvested and the labor behind them. She frequently referenced Rudolf Steiner's philosophy of farming and education, praising how much we were "learning and growing."

These orientations, spiritual overtones, philosophical conversations, and communal meals helped cultivate a culture of holistic performance. During routine periods, Penelope and the volunteers appeared aligned, and the daily work flowed smoothly as farmhands supported one another. Still, this performance was not without its occasional strain.

Helpers, Not Farmers

Penelope's maternal leadership, combined with her reliance on experienced farmhands to train newcomers, encouraged volunteers to see themselves less as "farmers" and more as "assistants" supporting her work. Penelope and the volunteers routinely used the term farmhand to describe their role. Yet it was clear they did not see themselves as "farmers" in the fuller sense of embodying the craft and long-term responsibility of agriculture, but rather as assistants supporting Penelope's vision. This identity was not necessarily negative. Most volunteers were not there to build agricultural careers. They came to escape home for the summer, earn college credit, pursue personal reflection, socialize, stay near a city, or, in one case, complete Peace Corps application requirements. Only a few were motivated primarily by farming itself.

Seeing themselves as assistants allowed volunteers to keep psychological distance from the farm's operations and focus on their own interests. This perspective, in turn, reinforced the farm's holistic performance culture, where personal exploration and social connection often took precedence over the agricultural output.

Violations and Resistance: Balancing "Free Will" and Precise Work

Although Penelope framed herself as our "mother" and encouraged a family-like culture, she occasionally slipped into the role of manager. These moments jolted the volunteers and disrupted the holistic performance we built together. Sometimes at breakfast or lunch, when work was piling up or productivity had slipped, she reminded us of the "contracts" we had signed on our first day. Our contracts were simply a one-page list of house and work rules. Whenever she said, "Remember, you all signed the contract," volunteers exchanged irritated glances. It felt like an appeal to formal authority that contradicted the relationship we believed we had with her. We did not work because of a contract. We worked because we respected Penelope and felt accountable to one other. We all felt that the necessary work got done, even if the process was sometimes uneven.

This dual role was especially difficult for Penelope because the farm depended on volunteer labor while still requiring consistent productivity. Penelope knew operations could not run without us, and she worried about pushing volunteers too hard. That tension surfaced one morning during a pep talk. After emphasizing the importance of "working efficiently and carefully," she quickly softened. "But you're all volunteers, so do what you want to do. Free will." Most of us smiled knowingly. Those who had been there longer understood she could not, and likely would not, enforce consequences if we ignored her requests.

Volunteers resisted most when their identity or routines felt threatened. Although Penelope assigned experienced farmhands to train newcomers, each trainer developed their own method, and instruction gradually became our domain rather than hers. New volunteers turned to other farmhands for tips, help, and reassurance. While Penelope had intentionally cultivated this peer structure, she still maintained precise expectations for how produce should be harvested and could not resist offering frequent suggestions.

As one farmhand put it, "Penelope was particular about the way she wanted everything done." She possessed genuine expertise, knowing how to cut kale at the base for the best appearance, which rubber bands to use to bundle different crops, how to cover greens with a cotton cloth in the sun, and how to bend your knees to avoid injury during seven-hour harvesting days. But volunteers often interpreted these interventions as unnecessary corrections. Responses ranged from vigorous nodding ("Okay, got it") to polite deflection ("Sure, I'll see what I can do") to mild annoyance ("I know").

Nearly everyone admitted to feeling irritated by the volume of suggestions. One said bluntly, "Penelope likes to micromanage and complain about our work." Another observed that "none of the [CSA] people complain about anything they pick up," so why change what was already working? In practice, farmhands rarely adjusted their technique after her recommendations.

Penelope confided in me that it upset her that "nobody listens... but what can I do?" She did not fully realize that by positioning herself as a nurturing mother and fostering a culture where volunteers relied primarily on one another, she had limited her ability to assert authority. At the same time, she hesitated to push harder for fear volunteers might withdraw their labor altogether. Her personal philosophy reinforced this restraint, rooted in the belief that volunteers should choose to learn and grow, experiencing the farm as a space for self-discovery rather than a workplace that demands compliance.

Free Will Meets Precision

Penelope had one primary strategy for getting volunteers to follow her preferred methods. She asked those she viewed as most responsible to "check on" the others' harvesting. The group of "responsible volunteers" included me, Aiko, and a hardworking but relatively new volunteer named Caitlin. The request immediately clashed with how we understood our relationships on the farm. Among volunteers, the norm was mutual respect and equal status. We helped and trained one another, but did not closely scrutinize one another's work. All three of us were uncomfortable stepping into a supervisory role.

Aiko, who had been on the farm the longest and openly aspired to a career in agriculture, was the only volunteer with meaningful informal authority. When Penelope asked her to relay instructions to volunteers who needed correction, she softened the message by attributing it to Penelope. "Penelope would like it if you...," or "It's not me, but Penelope asked if I could tell you...." Farmhands listened, not because the request originated with Penelope, but because it came from Aiko. Her reputation for diligence and expertise gave her credibility.

Still, Aiko resented being placed in this position. She told me, "It's not my job to tell them what to do. That's Penelope's job!" Eventually, after being asked too many times to intervene, Aiko confronted Penelope. Standing nearby, I heard her say, "I think it's better for you to tell them what you want them to do." Penelope responded with a meek "Okay." But when Penelope tried delivering suggestions herself, volunteers continued to resist. The routine we built, grounded in peer equality and distance from formal authority, left little room for Penelope to reassert control.

Performing Stability at Rolling Hills

Routine stability at Rolling Hills rested on a shared belief in "holistic work," but that shared language masked divergent interpretations. For Penelope, shaped by her farming philosophy and maternal self-understanding, holistic work meant learning by doing under her guidance and spiritual framing. For volunteers, it was filtered through personal goals, friendships, and communal living. They saw themselves as sustaining the CSA while building relationships and reflecting on life. "Holistic work" organized activity, but it carried distinct meanings for Penelope and the volunteers.

Stability endured not because Penelope exercised tight authority, but because volunteers developed dense peer interdependence. Rather than relying primarily on her direction, they trained one another, coordinated tasks collaboratively, and generated their own informal standards of competence. Over time, this horizontal coordination produced a sense of shared ownership over the farm's daily rhythm. When Penelope intervened too directly, her suggestions felt less like guidance and more like violations of a culture volunteers believed they had built.

Motivation flowed primarily through peer obligation rather than managerial control. Although occasional free riders emerged, Penelope had limited leverage to discipline them. Instead, volunteers enforced norms informally by excluding uncooperative members from social activities such as movie nights or trips to town. These small sanctions reinforced expectations about contribution and belonging. Social inclusion became the primary currency of accountability.

The durability of this system depended heavily on long-term volunteers, the "special souls," as Penelope referred to them, who stayed six months or more. They carried institutional knowledge, trained newcomers, and sustained the culture of interdependence. Without them, Penelope believed the farm would require more formal authority to function smoothly. Yet because she understood Rolling Hills as "a place of education as much as it is a business," formalization remained unlikely. Stability, therefore, rested on relational glue rather than formal controls, making it resilient in the short term but vulnerable to turnover.

AeroGears

Ostensive goal: A precise part
Routine stability performance: Stick to your task

Protection from Afar, Pressure Up Close

At AeroGears, routine stability centered on performing precision through task-based coordination. In practice, it required adhering to clearly defined roles so each part is produced accurately and efficiently. Stability emerged not from warmth or consensus but from disciplined role boundaries and a hierarchy that blended paternal protection with managerial fear. Stability required both technical precision and the visible performance of effort.

Employees worked under constant scrutiny from Jack, the floor manager. Workers worried not only about how they operated machinery, but also about how attentive or busy they appeared. Even small imperfections, or simply the perception of idleness, could draw rebuke. A machinist lingering too long at a workstation, pausing to chat, or appearing unhurried, risked correction. This vigilance created an atmosphere in which employees monitored not only their output but their visible performance of effort.

One long-time employee described this guarded dissatisfaction. When asked why he stayed at AeroGears, he smiled and said, "I like it." Then he added, "That's what I'll tell you, but that's not the truth." He clarified, "If there's a better opportunity out there, I would take it." Reflecting on Jack's feedback style, he explained, "You mostly hear feedback when you've done something wrong...Occasionally when something went well you'll get a 'good job,' but not too often." Another employee described Jack as "difficult to get along with." The careful phrasing reflected how reluctant many workers felt to voice concerns about him.

Even Leo, the company's owner, privately acknowledged Jack's negative impact. Leo told me, "I've had employees that have left this place, good employees, that have left because of Jack." When I asked why Jack remained, Leo replied, "Have you ever seen anyone work as hard as him? That's why I keep him...He's here early every morning, and on Saturdays, and is usually the last to leave...but I know he's a problem." Although Leo recognized Jack's role in poor retention, he chose not to intervene, allowing Jack's conduct to continue shaping shop-floor culture.

Outside consultants I spoke with noticed the same pattern. One suggested anger management counseling, while another joked that Jack "must have some sort of dirt on Leo" to explain his continued authority. Across the organization, it was widely understood that Jack's behavior, though disliked, carried implicit approval from Leo. In this system, hard work functioned as moral cover for interpersonal damage.

In contrast, employees spoke warmly about Leo. Many described him as a "good guy" and "a smart businessman." Leo often emphasized that he "hadn't fired anyone since 1983." During the 2008–2009 recession, he explained, "I didn't let anyone go," instead of cutting hours to protect jobs and even going into debt to pay employees. Workers remembered this period in paternal terms, saying Leo "really took care of us."

Despite this loyalty, Leo remained largely removed from daily operations. Jack controlled the emotional climate of the factory, shaping how employees interacted, stayed in their lanes, and focused narrowly on their tasks. While Leo symbolized protection and long-term security from a distance, Jack governed everyday work through pressure, correction, and the steady possibility of reprimand.

Stick to Your Task

From my desk upstairs, I often heard Jack's heavy steps on the staircase as he came up for coffee. Almost inevitably, he would complain that machinists were "not listening" or "not thinking." On the floor, I watched him reprimand employees for working too slowly, making mistakes, or machining the wrong part. Because every job had to pass through Jack before reaching the floor, workers interacted with him constantly, yet they tried to minimize unnecessary contact.

Machinists frequently had ideas for improving processing speed or part quality, and Alex, the quality manager, encouraged these suggestions because "they're the ones who know the process best." Any change, however, required Jack's approval. His dismissive facial expressions, curt comments, and unpredictable irritation signaled that deviation carried risk. As a result, employees rarely offered input.

More importantly, machinists avoided helping one another unless Jack explicitly assigned it. Although machinists were friendly with one another, eating lunch together, chatting before shifts, and taking smoking breaks, they kept their distance on the factory floor. Assisting a coworker risked drawing Jack's anger. As a result, daily performance narrowed to doing only the assigned task and avoiding attention.

When workers had questions and, on rare occasions, turned to one another for a quick answer, the response was usually, "Ask Jack." More often, they simply kept going, even when they suspected a part was imperfect. Problems surfaced only later, when Jack or a quality assurance assistant inspected the batch. Workers then claimed they "didn't notice" or that checking previous steps "wasn't their responsibility."

Jack's absence revealed how much inefficiency this culture produced. During one of Jack's infrequent and short vacations, Alex, who tracked job progress among other duties, discovered that the piece counts on a major order did not add up. Multiple machinists had miscounted their batches and passed them along without verification. No one double-checked the totals. To identify the root cause, Alex retraced hundreds of parts spread across more than a dozen sub-jobs. He emphasized that the mistakes weren't deliberate: "It's not done intentionally… They don't care about me. And frankly, I couldn't give a fuck what they do. But this is what I need to do when [Jack's] away."

From my perspective, a simple double-check could have prevented the error. But Alex reinforced the shop's culture by insisting it was not his role to change how machinists worked, only to uncover problems after the fact. The insistence on staying in one's lane preserved authority but weakened collective ownership.

This strict adherence to "stick to your task" generated recurring delays, rework, rushed orders, and wasted material. Yet it also reinforced the dominant stability performance at AeroGears, which emphasized minimizing risk, avoiding Jack's scrutiny, and focusing narrowly on one's own piece of the job, even at the expense of overall productivity.

Always Behind, Always Shipping Red

I quickly realized that many of the "complaints" Jack attributed to employees reflected legitimate concerns about meeting promised delivery dates, even though the machinists were not responsible for the delays.

One exchange captures the pattern. Jack recounted: "Jon [a machinist] said this to me three times in the last two days, 'I'm just trying to keep up.'" Jack said he responded, "If you're behind, just do your job. If you're behind, that's fine because *we're* behind."

This reassurance implied that delays were not attributable to the machinists. But Jack frequently reprimanded workers for moving too slow, creating rework, or contributing to production bottlenecks. I regularly watched him raise his voice at employees who were idle for only a few moments. Workers would explain that they were waiting on a part from another machine, but Jack would scold them about how far "behind" the shop was and then assign them a completely different job to fill the gap.

This practice compounded delays. Once machinists began the new assignment, they continued machining those parts until Jack explicitly told them to switch back. What appeared to be decisive intervention often multiplied unfinished work.

These moments revealed missed opportunities to reshape the shop's performance. Rather than encouraging machinists to coordinate with one another or anticipate downstream needs, Jack reinforced the routine of sticking strictly to assigned tasks. By personally redistributing work whenever a delay surfaced, he ensured that workflow decisions continued to funnel through him. Stability was maintained not by solving delays but by centralizing control over them.

Two newer management hires, Keith, the Assistant Project Manager, and Fred, the Assistant Floor Manager, both seasoned factory men, were stunned by the financial consequences of this dysfunction. Their chief grievance was the staggering amount spent on "UPS Red," a common shorthand for expensive, overnight shipping. In my final months, I repeatedly heard the question, "Should we ship it Red?"

AeroGears used UPS Red not only to send finished parts to customers but also to rush batches back and forth between outside heat-treat and chemical-treat facilities. Some jobs were shipped Red three separate times before reaching the final client. One week, Keith walked me through his calculations. Over the previous five days alone, the factory had spent an additional $3,000 on overnight shipping. Exasperated, he asked, "How can we recoup these losses? There's no way. I'd rather figure out a way to save the company money so I can get a raise."

The shop remained locked in a familiar pattern, marked by fragmented tasks, minimal cooperation, constant fire drills, and a steady rhythm of falling behind and shipping everything Red.

Even Leaders Must Stay in Their Lane

Unlike Rolling Hills, where resistance flowed upward from volunteers, AeroGears employees rarely pushed back against the routine stability performance.

Workers who resisted were typically scolded into compliance or eventually left the company. As several machinists told me, they "did not feel appreciated" but stayed only because they could not find steady work elsewhere. One described himself as a "lifer," not out of loyalty but out of limited options.

Most resistance at AeroGears surfaced not from the shop floor but within management, particularly around control over job sequencing and workflow priorities. Jack, Leo, and Alex all complained that "everyone's doing the same job," by which they meant that multiple managers were making decisions about which orders should run first, which parts should be rushed, and how jobs should move through the factory. Ironically, leadership embodied the very expectation it demanded of machinists. Stick to your task. Deviations, especially around job scheduling, was treated as a violation.

These violations produced open friction. A common sequence unfolded like this. Alex handed a job to Jack, who authorized its release to the floor. The next day, Leo received a call from a customer requesting a rush order. Without consulting Jack, Leo went directly to the floor and instructed a machinist to prioritize the rushed part. Later, when Jack discovered the original job unfinished, his voice rose. He demanded to know why the machinist had switched tasks. The machinist replied simply, "Leo told me to work on this one instead."

When I asked workers why they didn't check with Jack before switching, their answer was straightforward: "Leo is the owner, so what he says goes." Within AeroGears' culture of unquestioned task completion, following Leo's instruction made perfect sense.

Jack saw it differently. He believed he controlled the factory floor and viewed Leo's interventions as encroachments on his authority. Rather than working around the disruption, he confronted Leo directly, telling him not to interfere. The exchanges were tense and clipped, sometimes unfolding in front of employees. In these moments, Jack treated Leo as the one violating routine operations. Even at the top of the hierarchy, sticking to one's task remained a governing norm, and Jack expected Leo to abide by it.

The Magical Yellow Pad

One of the clearest expressions of Jack's authority, and his resistance to organizational change, was his reliance on a yellow legal pad to schedule all shop-floor work. AeroGears routinely had dozens of jobs in process, each requiring different machines, machinist skill levels, and material certifications. Some aerospace parts could only be cut on approved machines, meaning if a machine was tied up with another job, boxes of parts sat waiting for hours or even days. These bottlenecks cascaded across the factory, delaying multiple jobs at once. Coordinating this flow was extraordinarily complex.

Computerized scheduling systems have existed for decades and can easily manage variables such as machine availability, estimated cut times, skill levels, employee vacation time, shift overlaps, and many other factors. AeroGears even purchased a software designed precisely to solve these problems. In fact, Leo had brought me on board in part, to help install, learn, and then train staff on the new software.

Despite owning the software for more than eight years, Jack controlled all scheduling through what Keith jokingly called "that magical yellow pad." Everyone knew the pad. It functioned as the central nervous system of the shop. Jack carried it across the floor, checking jobs and making updates with layer upon layer of whiteout. If a part originally assigned to one machine was moved to another, he whited out the old entry and rewrote it. That single, heavily corrected pad directed hundreds of thousands of dollars of work each day.

No one else was permitted to update it. If a machinist, manager, or even Leo wanted to know the status of a job, they had to ask Jack. He alone possessed the information, captured in tight, handwritten notes on what everyone half-joked, half-feared was the factory's "magic" scheduling tool.

The pad was not a relic of outdated training or technological resistance. It was a mechanism of control. By maintaining sole authority over the production schedule, Jack centralized job sequencing.

Performing Stability at AeroGears

Routine stability at AeroGears was organized around concentrated authority and task isolation. Jack's management of production through his "magical yellow pad" centralized informational power and structured work around a strict norm of sticking to your task. This arrangement limited coordination but produced predictability. Because only Jack possessed complete scheduling visibility, machinists operated within narrow boundaries, avoiding cross-assistance to prevent reprimand. Collaboration was not expected, and avoidance became rational.

Long-term employees, though often frustrated, helped sustain this system. Many felt unappreciated but believed AeroGears offered more security than other factories in the region. Their gratitude toward Leo, who they believed had "kept everyone working" through the recession, combined with limited alternatives, made endurance more rational than confrontation. The routine persisted not because workers endorsed Jack's behavior, but because challenging it carried risk.

Jack's rule through discipline and fear discouraged collaboration. Friends at lunch became isolated workers on the floor, avoiding even small acts of assistance to prevent reprimand for touching a job that "wasn't theirs." Avoidance was widely seen as the logical response to "Jack's attitude." For many machinists, exit rather than voice appeared to be the only viable form of resistance.

At the management level, frustration surfaced differently. Alex described "the general culture of 'No'" at AeroGears, his shorthand for the resistance he encountered when he attempted to create processes that would allow the company to function if "Jack or Leo suddenly died." Without institutionalized systems, knowledge remained concentrated and fragile. Yet Leo and Jack favored narrowly defined roles that preserved authority over scalability.

Routine stability at AeroGears produced predictability and role clarity, but at the cost of institutional learning. The system functioned as long as its central figures remained in place. In this way, stability was not neutral. It protected concentrated power while constraining organizational resilience.

Chapter 7

Who's in Charge?

ElderCare

Ostensive goal: Compassionate care
Routine stability performance: Collaborative effort

Balancing Gray and Black-and-White

At ElderCare, routine stability emerged not from strict hierarchy or rigid role boundaries but from ongoing negotiation between two leaders whose contrasting styles shaped everyday coordination. In practice, that required working together to ensure clients receive consistent, attentive support across shifting schedules and needs. Rather than relying on formal authority, order was sustained through conversation, mutual adjustment, and shared interpretation of what good care required.

Alice often explained that she started ElderCare to create the kind of workplace she wanted to be part of. After years in adversarial, rigid corporate environments, she envisioned a culture in which people "really liked each other," creativity mattered, and decisions were not simply handed down from above. As she put it, she did not want a workplace where someone made a decision and "you just had to follow the plan and zooooom," mimicking a plane taking off. Instead, she valued flexibility, input, and collaboration.

Together with Jenn and a small office staff, Alice affectionately described her employees as "a ragtag team." Even as the organization grew, its core culture remained relational rather than hierarchical, with the office team shaping ElderCare's daily rhythm and identity.

At the heart of this stability was the leadership partnership between Alice and Jenn. Although Alice owned the business and Jenn served as administrative assistant, they operated in many ways as co-leaders. Alice emphasized how their contrasting styles strengthened the business: "Most [franchisees] have high turnover in [the administrative assistant] position…

DOI: 10.4324/9781003779803-9

but I think [Jenn stayed because] Jenn and I complement each other very well. Jenn's more black and white, and I'm more gray. Right Jenn?" Jenn replied, "Oh, yes. Very gray. Gray, gray, gray." Alice added, "I go through all the possibilities...It can get annoying." Jenn simply nodded. Their dynamic paired expansive thinking with clarity and decisiveness.

Decision-making unfolded through quick, informal exchanges rather than formal processes. Alice often talked through scenarios aloud, weighing options, while Jenn distilled what mattered most, offered her recommendation, and concluded with "Done," "That was easy," or "That was a no-brainer." ElderCare's coordination depended less on formal procedures and more on these exchanges, which were rapid, relational, and trust-based.

Alice regularly sought Jenn's input on hiring, reprimanding caregivers, and matching caregivers with clients, even joking about Jenn's role: "Everyone knows what to do, which is everything." Their overlapping responsibilities occasionally blurred accountability. When ElderCare's part-time home health consultant stopped by the office and asked Jenn which aide would be sent to a client, Jenn replied, "Ask Alice." Alice responded, "It's up to Jenn." Frustrated, the consultant pressed, "Are you two going to ever figure out who's responsible for what?" Neither answered. The exchange captured both the flexibility and fragility of shared authority, revealing its tradeoffs.

Both Alice and Jenn found meaning in their work, though in different ways. Jenn joked that her favorite part was "Going home at night," then added, "My favorite part is when the elderlies call me and need help and I can help them...That makes me feel warm and fuzzy inside." She followed up this positive account with an acknowledgement of the emotional strain: "And then I'll get a phone call from someone else who yells at me and says bad things about me."

Alice, by contrast, loved "going out there and meeting the people I'm helping." Jenn preferred helping "from afar," explaining that seeing clients' conditions "depresses me." When Alice once asked Jenn to do an in-home assessment, Jenn said, "I don't want to. I don't like to." Alice replied, "This is the only nice thing about this business!" Jenn asked, "What is?" Alice said, "Sitting in someone's living room and talking to them. Everything else isn't worth it."

Despite these differences in approach, both were anchored in the same underlying value of helping others. That commitment shaped daily work, from carefully matching aides to clients to offering emotional support for elderly patients and shared frustration when families neglected their relatives. ElderCare's culture was sustained less by formal structures than by relationships, humor, and mutual respect. During routine stability, coordination emerged not from rigid systems but from trust and a shared sense of purpose. Stability rested on relational alignment rather than procedural enforcement.

Humor as Coordination

Life inside the ElderCare office was marked by a mix of exasperation and humor, colored by daily encounters with unpredictable aides, demanding clients, and complex family dynamics. Alice often joked that the office ran "on a wing and a prayer."

On one particularly chaotic day, a caregiver was reported for falling asleep at a senior daycare center, others skipped required training, and no one could cover a last-minute weekend shift. By mid-afternoon, Alice was exasperated:

> It is beyond me that at 3:00 p.m. today, this one falls asleep, this one can't come in to do her training…and this one says, "Ohhh, I just don't want to"…we just don't have enough aides or enough cases to play with this shit.

Moments later, the aide who had fallen asleep on the job texted an explanation: "The reason I think that I knotted out was that… they were giving out huge hot dogs and sodas for lunch…and fatty foods makes you tired… and I usually eats two pieces of fruit for lunch or a healthy sandwich…" After pointing out the mistypes, Alice read the message aloud, laughing. "Who would ever think of texting your boss like that?" She continued:

> You know, my dad warned me about this business. He said, "Alice, you will not be able to relate to these people." And I said, in my infinite wisdom, "I've worked with warehouse people, I can relate." You know what, I can't.

Despite often joking about not connecting with her aides, Alice learned to work with them effectively. She rewarded basic competence, attributed many struggles to social circumstances rather than individual shortcomings and turned frustration into humor. On especially chaotic days, she called ElderCare "an island of misfit toys," likening the workforce to the abandoned characters from *Rudolph the Red-Nosed Reindeer*. Beneath the sarcasm was pride in keeping the organization running despite constant challenges.

In this way, humor functioned as a coordination mechanism, converting frustration into relational cohesion. It relieved stress, helped process the emotional weight of elder care, and, most importantly, became an informal system for sharing information. Through jokes and storytelling, Alice and Jenn exchanged updates about aide reliability, client needs, and emerging problems, allowing the office to stay aligned without formal reporting structures.

This dynamic was most visible in scheduling, the office's most critical collaborative task. Although Jenn initially managed it, and later a part-time specialist assisted, everyone contributed insight about which caregivers could handle difficult clients, weekend shifts, or emotionally demanding cases. While much of the administrative workload revolved around billing and paperwork, matching aides to clients remained meaningful shared labor that directly advanced ElderCare's goal of compassionate care.

Not all collaboration, however, carrier the same value. A full-time nurse frequently required help with basic technology, including faxing, scanning, and even logging into the system. While she viewed these requests as routine, others experienced them as draining and misaligned with the office's priorities. Unlike scheduling support, this assistance did not enhance patient care. It generated irritation rather than solidarity.

At ElderCare, collaboration was selective rather than indiscriminate. Helping was expected, but only when it contributed to what the team defined as good care. Humor and shared problem-solving organized daily work, strengthened relationships, and sustained the organization under constant pressure. Yet collective effort was reserved for tasks that advanced the company's goal, reflecting a culture that balanced compassion with clear expectations about competence and contribution.

Pride in the Work, Strain in the Schedule

In interviews, most home health aides described caring for elderly clients was their primary motivation. Many expressed genuine pride in their work and believed they possessed a particular temperament suited to the role. At the same time, the field attracted workers because licensing was relatively quick, inexpensive, and flexible. Some preferred morning shifts so they could care for their own children in the afternoon, while others worked weekends to accommodate additional jobs during the week.

Despite this commitment, reliability remained a persistent challenge. Many aides lacked dependable transportation in ElderCare's suburban service area, where limited public transit often left them miles from clients' homes. Even those with cars regularly faced mechanical problems. Others accepted new assignments only to cancel days later after securing better-paying or longer-term work elsewhere. These last-minute changes forced the office into constant rescheduling and generated daily operational strain.

Alice understood that many of these challenges were endemic to the home health care industry and reflected broader labor-market realities. High turnover, transportation barriers, and competing caregiving responsibilities were common across agencies serving similar workforces. The one issue Alice treated as individual and inexcusable was lateness. As Alice put it,

> If you're supposed to be somewhere on time, you need to be there on time. And when [I] get angry at someone for being late, they don't get it. It's like, "What did I do wrong?" because they're probably doing something at home for their own children or their own elderly parent or a neighbor, and they think it's okay if they're a little late.

Even loyal aides occasionally arrived late, and because clients rarely complained, Alice often learned of the delay only when she called the home herself.

For Alice and Jenn, managing reliability was less about strict punishment than navigating economic precarity, competing obligations, and the emotional demands of care work. Punctuality became not just an operational requirement but a moral boundary. Maintaining it required steady communication, relational repair, and clear expectations to keep the organization functioning smoothly.

When Care Crosses a Line

Another recurring challenge at ElderCare involved male clients who behaved inappropriately toward female caregivers. A nurse referred to these clients as "horn dogs," while Jenn called them "dirty old men." Complaints typically arose during intimate care tasks, such as bathing or helping clients with changing clothes, when some men made suggestive comments or asked aides to "go to bed" with them.

Most aides handled these incidents with humor, aware that the clients' frailty made any physical escalation unlikely. In rare cases involving threats, usually from patients with dementia, ElderCare immediately removed aides from the home and recommended placement in a full-time care facility. While many aides brushed off flirtation, others felt genuinely uncomfortable. When concerns were raised, reassignment followed. One caregiver in particular was never again placed with clients whom Alice and the head nurse considered "a little too flirty."

For Alice and her team, managing inappropriate client behavior required balancing employee well-being, client dignity, and operational continuity. Compassion did not mean permissiveness. The office culture treated these situations seriously, even when humor helped staff cope with the awkward realities of intimate care work.

Feeling Undervalued, Taking More

Despite Jenn's strong intrinsic motivation and pride in helping clients, she increasingly resented what she viewed as inadequate compensation. She often stayed late, brought work home, and told me, "I don't get paid enough to handle all this," insisting she deserved more for "all the anxiety this job gives me." Jenn understood ElderCare's financial constraints. She managed payroll and accounts receivable and knew the company was not consistently profitable, but she still believed her compensation did not reflect the scope of her responsibilities.

When Jenn temporarily drove aides to client homes, she gave herself a weekly pay increase to cover gas and vehicle expenses. After she stopped driving, she continued paying herself the additional amount. She admitted she knew this violated standard procedure but felt she "deserved it" and would continue "until Alice said otherwise." Alice later told the part-time consultant, who relayed to me, that "I didn't tell her she could do that." But Alice chose not to confront Jenn because she did not want to "stir things up."

Like Leo's tolerance of Jack at AeroGears, Alice prioritized relational stability over financial clarity. By avoiding the confrontation, she implicitly accepted the pay increase in order to preserve collaboration. The partnership between Alice and Jenn remained intact, but unresolved compensation tensions gradually eroded the culture of trust and fairness they had built.

Performing Stability at ElderCare

Routine stability at ElderCare rested on collaborative coordination grounded in shared meaning rather than formal hierarchy. Alice deliberately hired staff with complementary skills and personalities, building what she described as a workplace she "wanted to come to every day." Daily operations revolved around matching caregivers with clients, a task guided less by formal metrics than by accumulated stories. Staff exchanged narratives of frustration, humor, and experience, using them to refine judgments about which caregiver would fit which household.

Humor served both practical and emotional functions. Employees joked about chronically late aides operating on their own timeline, "dirty old men" who flirted during intimate care, and families who neglected aging relatives. These stories lightened the emotional weight of elder care while simultaneously circulating tacit knowledge that improved further decision-making. Even when Alice laughed about the "stupidity of this business," as she put it, she reaffirmed the deeper meaning she found in helping clients and cultivating a supportive office culture.

Collaboration was valued when it advanced care. Experience-based input strengthened scheduling decisions. Asking others to absorb ordinary responsibilities risked violating the norm of mutual contribution. A subtler breach emerged around compensation. Feeling that her contributions were undervalued, Jenn compensated herself with an unauthorized weekly supplement. Alice chose not to confront her. Rather than asserting formal authority, she preserved relational equilibrium, treating trust as more essential to stability than procedural clarity.

ElderCare's routine stability performance therefore depended on trust, humor, and a shared commitment to compassionate care. But this relational flexibility also absorbed unresolved tensions. Stability endured not because roles were rigidly defined, but because differences were managed informally and conflicts were softened rather than structurally resolved.

Thorny Rose

Ostensive goal: Beautiful arrangements
Routine stability performance: Whatever needs to get done

Care Without Authority, Control Without Trust

At Thorny Rose, routine stability did not rest on settled authority or clearly defined role boundaries, but on a fragile equilibrium among competing leadership styles and family loyalties. In practice, this translated into fluid roles, with each sibling stepping in wherever gaps appeared to keep the shop running.

From the customer counter, the store appeared to operate without a clear leader. That absence of visible authority was not inherently dysfunctional, but it gave the shop a chaotic, improvisational feel. Activity unfolded in bursts. Employees asked whoever was nearby for answers. Decisions were made on the fly.

Internally, however, leadership was far from absent. Julian carried the heaviest share of responsibility. He handled most customer disputes, legal and financial matters, wholesale relationships, and complex floral arrangements. When deliveries ran late or paperwork piled up, he sighed that "[my family] dropped the ball again," adding that they "get lazy" and assume "it just magically gets done." Even routine administrative tasks returned to his desk when others didn't complete the work. "My family's just not reliable sometimes," he admitted.

Julian often joked about what happened in his absence. When customers called with billing questions, Tyler would say, "The office manager is not in today, can you call back tomorrow?" Julian teased, "I never showed you where the file cabinet is?" She brushed it off: "I'm tired, I'm going home." Julian noted that he had shown them, but "nobody does the work." Over time, he became the default manager of every department.

Yet when he spent time paying bills or meeting with the accountant, his siblings accused him of "just sitting around." When Tyler once asked if he was "going to get off your ass and help make arrangements," Julian snapped, "If I don't take care of this, who's going to pay the electric bill? When there's no lights in the morning, what's going to happen then?" She had no response.

Nevertheless, his siblings did recognize his contributions. Nicholas said, "Julian probably does 80 percent of what's needed here." Lilia called him "a saint." Tyler admitted, "I don't know what would happen if Julian wasn't here." Gratitude, however, did not translate into authority. There was no formal hierarchy, and Julian struggled to direct others' work. He contrasted himself with his father, who "ran the shop like a dictator."

"I'm the father, but no one listens to me," Julian said. He attributed this to his "abandonment issues," rooted in his father leaving the family when the siblings were very young children and Julian was a teenager. Having stepped into a caretaking role early in life, he found it difficult to enforce accountability now. His loyalty to family made confrontation feel like betrayal rather than management.

Julian repeatedly asked his siblings to handle billing, taxes, and legal tasks, often providing detailed instructions. The work was rarely completed. "You should never have family work for you because you can't tell them what to do," he said. Yet the siblings remained in the business out of loyalty to their family legacy, while Julian continued carrying the administrative burden, sacrificing personal time and accumulating resentment over their inconsistent follow-through.

Alongside Julian, Nicholas functioned as the other dominant leader. He managed non-family employees, oversaw physically demanding operations, and moved through the shop with relentless speed. His style, however, contrasted sharply with Julian's patience. Some siblings called him "a tyrant." Convinced that people were inherently lazy, Nicholas relied on close monitoring, micromanagement, and frequent yelling to keep work moving.

The tension surfaced one summer when employees repeatedly left a greenhouse door open, damaging flowers. After multiple reminders, Nicholas exploded: "Julian, this shit has to change. Now they're laughing when I tell them to keep the door closed. You being nice to everyone leads me to have to yell at everyone." Julian replied evenly, "I tell them what they need to do." Nicholas shot back, "No, but you let them get away with it...then I'm the asshole and nobody listens." Julian shrugged, turned away, and laughed. "Nicholas yells because he likes to yell, not because of me."

Together, Julian and Nicholas enacted competing leadership logics. One centered on caretaking without authority, and the other on control without trust. Their dynamic produced a workplace where responsibility was uneven, accountability fragile, and authority perpetually negotiated. Leadership flowed less from formal titles than from family history, emotional loyalties, and accumulated obligation. Thorny Rose held together not because authority was settled, but because the siblings remained bound by legacy and necessity, even as the terms of control remained unresolved.

Making Things Beautiful

At Thorny Rose, family identity was inseparable from floristry. The siblings took pride in the shop's eighty-year history and frequently invoked that legacy with customers. Nicholas framed it as their competitive advantage. "Do you know what our family is really good at?" he told me. "We make shit look beautiful and nobody would know the difference. I can make it beautiful."

When Tyler objected, "it's not shit," Nicholas clarified, "That's my point. To the average person looking at a flower in isolation, they would think that it's junk. But we know how to prune it, rearrange it, and organize it to make it look great." Tyler agreed, "That's true. We do that well."

This shared belief distinguished the family from competitors and reinforced their confidence in high-volume, high-pressure work. As Nicholas put it, people imagine florists as "women gently arranging flowers in a vase," but "we'd never make any money that way."

Skill at Thorny Rose was acquired through immersion rather than formal instruction. Although responsibilities were specialized, all siblings were expected to handle any customer who walked through the door. New situations were tackled first and critiqued afterward. I watched Tyler navigate a wedding consultation she felt unprepared to manage. Afterward, Lilia walked her through the interaction step by step, telling her she had done "good work... and you'll now know for next time." Tyler admitted she felt "uncomfortable doing it" and frustrated at being critiqued for something she had never been formally taught. Yet this trial-and-feedback approach was the norm.

Nicholas was explicit about the philosophy: "The only way to learn is to do it yourself." On my first day, he handed me a phone and an order pad, pointed to the credit card machine, and offered only brief guidance about occasions, budgets, and delivery. Unsure about pricing, I frequently put customers on hold to consult Julian or Nicholas, worried more about embarrassment than lost sales. After each call, Nicholas coached me on pricing and phrasing, suggesting lines like: "We guarantee that she'll love it" and "Our new flower order just arrived today." Training had no clearly defined timeline. Missed opportunities were tolerated, but improvement was expected.

This sink-or-swim logic applied across the shop. Siblings and seasonal workers cleaned flowers, built arrangements, managed deliveries, assembled balloon arrangements, prepared fruit baskets, and assisted walk-in customers. Everyone learned by doing. The result was a workforce that was flexible and resilient in production and service tasks, while administrative responsibilities remained concentrated in Julian's hands.

At Thorny Rose, expertise was not codified in manuals or systems. It lived in people, shaped by family history, shared stories, and repetition. Skills were acquired through participation and critique rather than formal instruction. The challenge was cultivating capability without burnout and confidence without resentment.

Find Something and Do It

At Thorny Rose, work was largely self-assigned. Everyone helped walk-in customers, answered phones, and built arrangements. Nicholas concentrated on wholesale accounts and seasonal sales, Lilia managed weddings, and Julian carried the administrative backbone of bills, taxes, insurance, flower orders, and payroll. Yet Julian was constantly pulled back into production and customer problems, leaving back-office responsibilities delayed not from neglect, but because immediate demands always took precedence.

The shop used a simple paper system to organize orders, with thirty-one clear plastic boxes lining the wall behind the counter, each labeled for a day of the month. Orders were sorted into these bins so upcoming work was visible to everyone. Julian encouraged the team to look ahead, starting complex arrangements early and prepare for heavy delivery days. In practice, he was usually the only one who did this. The others focused on the task directly in front of them. The culture rewarded responsiveness more than foresight.

On a typical day, three siblings worked alongside two delivery drivers and a full-time designer, whom Nicholas called Junior, a nickname that underscored both his youth and Nicholas's authority. The drivers did far more than deliver flowers. They answered phones, cleaned and watered plants, swept the shop, reorganized supplies, managed stock, inflated balloons, picked up food and coffee, and stepped in wherever needed. Nicholas or Julian typically assigned tasks, but when both were occupied, Tyler was asked to "give them something to do." Often unsure what to delegate, she sometimes assigned unproductive tasks (like rearranging vases that were recently rearranged) simply to project decisiveness and preserve authority.

This flexible system kept the shop moving, especially during peak seasons. The prevailing mindset was that nothing was "not my job." Yet the same adaptability that sustained daily operations also deferred long-term planning and administrative discipline. At Thorny Rose, priorities were clear and rarely questioned. The customer came first, today's orders had to be finished, and the doors had to stay open. Everything else could wait.

When Everything Becomes an Argument

At Thorny Rose, verbal conflict was routine rather than exceptional. From my first day, each sibling warned me that daily arguments were simply part of the business and that I would need a "tough skin" to work there. Although I was rarely the target, the constant back-and-forth created an emotionally charged atmosphere that made staff retention difficult. In the lead-up to Valentine's Day, one seasonal worker quit on her second day. As Julian explained, "she said that she couldn't take everyone yelling at each other and she couldn't work here anymore." He laughed as he told the story. The siblings joked that the reason they kept Junior, the only full-time non-family employee, was because "he's partially deaf." Nicholas even suggested everyone should have one fight each morning "to get out their resentments or whatever," though in truth the arguing never paused.

These clashes stemmed less from personal animosity than from competing interpretations of how work should be done. Julian prioritized administrative order and careful customer service. Nicholas pushed for speed and output. Tyler wanted to educate customers, while Lilia worried that too much instruction would encourage do-it-yourself arrangements and cut into sales. Without a shared definition of what "whatever needs to get done" meant, each sibling viewed the others as violating implicit expectations. Conflict, in this sense, was not a breakdown of routine stability but one of its defining features.

Unsolicited feedback became the clearest signal of those violations. Comments filled with "should," "could," and "ought" quickly triggered defensiveness and counter-critique. What began as advice often felt personal, turning constant evaluation into a source of irritation rather than improvement.

Even ordinary habits drew scrutiny. Tyler was frequently teased for taking breaks. One day, after returning with food, Nicholas said, "How about I just eat what you got there and you go back to work." Tyler replied, "But you ain't eating from my plate," and began eating faster. Nicholas smiled and said, "Just sit down and eat. Take your time." Tyler shot back, "Nicholas, I was out for like, two seconds [to get my food]." The exchange ended with smiles, but the humor carried an undercurrent of monitoring and judgment.

When teasing edged toward discomfort, someone would add, "I'm kidding. It was a joke," or "Don't take everything so seriously." Julian often reassured me, "Don't mind our little quips," and when exchanges became more pointed, he would say, "What happens at Thorny Rose, stays in Thorny Rose." In practice, conflict moved easily between work and family life.

As an outsider, I learned not to appear to "take sides." Nicholas once joked that I was "attached to Julian's umbilical cord," implying bias. Over time, I learned to read the room before responding, distinguishing between teasing meant as bonding and teasing delivered as critique. Learning that difference became a survival skill at Thorny Rose.

For leaders, Thorny Rose illustrates how unclear expectations, overlapping authority, and unresolved roles can normalize conflict. What the family experienced as honesty and banter often felt hostile to outsiders and exhausting to employees. Without shared standards for what "good work" required, everyday interactions became a continuous site of negotiation and emotional strain.

Because My Dad Always Said...

Although the siblings' father had died five years earlier, his influence remained embedded in the daily life of Thorny Rose. He had left the family when the children were young, yet Julian and Nicholas later worked alongside him as young adults, and all of the siblings spoke of him with respect. Nicholas revered his father's "good business sense" and his willingness to "do whatever is needed for the business." His presence endured not through written rules but through constant references to what he would have done or said.

Invoking their father's name served a strategic function. When siblings sought to reinforce standards, demand greater effort, or settle disagreements, they framed their position as something he had taught them. These were not nostalgic recollections. When a sibling began, "Because my dad always said...," conversation typically stopped. No one challenged the point. The remembered voice of their father became the final word.

His legacy also shaped customer interactions, signaling empathy, tradition, and legitimacy. References to family history strengthened relationships while reinforcing Thorny Rose's identity as a multigenerational business rooted in care. Even when the invocation seemed unnecessary, it added symbolic weight and credibility.

In this way, their father functioned as an informal moral and operational authority long after his death. His memory guided decisions, enforced standards, and shaped meaning in everyday work. Rather than relying on formal hierarchy, the siblings drew on shared history and symbolic authority to govern behavior, often more powerfully than titles or rules.

Below are excerpts from my notes showing how the phrase "my father" reinforced norms and shaped action:

On Accountability During Mistakes

When Tyler laughed after a small error during a stressful shift, Nicholas said, "If dad was here, you wouldn't be laughing about it."

On Solving Problems with Limited Resources

When Tyler ran out of purple flowers required by a family for a funeral arrangement, Julian advised, "Do what your father said. Make something beautiful instead."

On Reliability During Peak Seasons

When I was sneezing and coughing during a shift in early February, Tyler told me, "My father would say that you don't get sick until after Valentine's Day."

On Minimizing Customer Conflict

When there was uncertainty about whether a delivery was incomplete, Nicholas said, "My father would say that you shouldn't bring it to the attention of the customer. Only if they complain should we do something about it."

On the Fragility of Life

When funeral clients spoke about sudden loss, Julian often replied, "As my father would say, you never know what tomorrow will bring." He sometimes added, "God willing," explaining that his father believed, "You never know what could happen on any given day."

Guaranteeing Beauty

At Thorny Rose, creating beautiful arrangements was not simply an artistic aspiration. It was a business strategy. The siblings believed their competitive advantage rested on two commitments: striking design and strong value for customers' money. Long-standing supplier relationships allowed them to secure quality flowers at favorable prices, reinforcing that promise.

Beauty alone, however, was insufficient. Many customers ordered arrangements they would never see, sending flowers to grieving families, distant relatives, or colleagues. In these moments, uncertainty was high and trust had to be established quickly. The siblings relied on a familiar set of phrases that became part of the shop's everyday language. These expressions reassured customers, projected confidence, and signaled professionalism. Over time, they were woven into routine operations, spoken almost automatically regardless of who took the order.

These phrases were more than just customer service scripts. They functioned as cultural tools, translating the family's pride, experience, and reputation into trust. Common refrains included:

"We'll take care of you."
"I guarantee it'll be beautiful."
"That'll make her feel really special."
"I assure you it's going to wow her."
"Just let the flowers say it all."
"It's my brothers and sisters that work here, so any of us will take really good care of you."

To the siblings, this language did not feel rehearsed. As Tyler explained, they did not say these things "to try to convince anyone that they should buy from us." In this way, reassurance became part of the work itself. It was a routine performance that turned uncertainty into trust and strengthened Thorny Rose's identity as a family business that creates meaning for others.

Performing Stability at Thorny Rose

At Thorny Rose, routine stability rested on a shared commitment to sustaining the multigenerational business, even as daily operations were marked by persistent conflict. The guiding logic was "do whatever needs to get done," but each sibling interpreted that mandate differently. Julian expected more help with legal, tax, and billing work. Nicholas believed stricter discipline would improve employee performance and reduce confrontation. Tyler saw herself as meeting expectations within a narrower scope. These mismatched assumptions produced violations of expectation, fueling raised voices, emotional strain, and ongoing "family drama."

Conflict did not derail operations because it was normalized. Rather than formally clarifying authority or reconciling expectations, the siblings relied on an inherited moral anchor. Invoking their father's name and recalling "what Dad would have said" functioned as symbolic authority that could halt arguments when direct leadership faltered. His remembered voice became an informal governance system, a shared reference point no sibling openly contested. In moments of impasse, the past stabilized the present.

Despite the turbulence, Thorny Rose consistently delivered high-quality floral work. Shared expertise, reinforced through critique and hands-on learning, sustained craft standards and ensured any sibling could step in to complete an arrangement when needed. Familiar customer-facing phrases signaled reliability, craftsmanship, and value. Pride in their skill and in the family legacy sustained performance even when relationships were strained.

Yet the long-term costs of unresolved tension were visible. Over time, Lilia reduced her involvement to two days per week, supplementing her income through wedding consultations. Julian absorbed increasing administrative responsibility. The shop continued to operate, but its stability depended heavily on uneven labor and emotional endurance. Thorny Rose's future rested less on floral expertise than on whether the siblings could align expectations, share authority, and lessen the relational toll embedded in their everyday rhythm.

Chapter 8

The Logic of Stability

Leading When Nothing Is on Fire

Across Rolling Hills, AeroGears, ElderCare, and Thorny Rose, leaders and employees created organizational order with limited financial, human, and social capital. Coordination did not depend primarily on formal systems or carefully engineered strategy. It developed through patterned interaction, informal relationships, and shared ways of pursuing simple ostensive goals. Order was not engineered from above. It was enacted through everyday practice. Stability endured through repeated exchanges, shared expectations, and taken-for-granted norms that guided daily work.

Leadership approaches varied sharply. Only one leader, Alice at ElderCare, intentionally sought to shape culture by hiring staff who reinforced a collaborative and supportive environment. In contrast, Penelope at Rolling Hills accepted nearly any volunteer who expressed interest in work. Although Penelope articulated a clear philosophy about how the farm should operate, she struggled to enforce her vision, and volunteers developed their own interpretations of appropriate work behavior.

At AeroGears, Leo recognized that Jack's confrontational style damaged morale and retention, but he chose not to intervene. At Thorny Rose, culture was never consciously managed. With four siblings as the core workforce, authority remained fluid, family history shaped decisions, and personal dynamics blurred professional boundaries.

Despite these differences in leadership style and structure, all four firms achieved routine stability.

Each organization developed a distinct idioculture shaped by history, relationships, and shared meaning. At Rolling Hills, learning occurred through immersion. Volunteers absorbed norms by watching Aiko, whose informal authority allowed mild defiance to become normalized. At AeroGears, resistance carried consequences. Machinists narrowed their focus to assigned tasks, initiative faded, and long-tenured loyalty replaced voice. At ElderCare, collaboration was sustained through storytelling, as staff circulated emotionally charged client experiences that reinforced purpose and standards. At Thorny Rose, family teasing and the symbolic

DOI: 10.4324/9781003779803-10

authority of "my father" structured daily interaction, while non-family employees struggled to access that shared moral reference point.

These cultures generated both strengths and inefficiencies. Across firms, new members learned not through formal onboarding but through observation, participation, and correction. Stability rested on taken-for-granted norms that defined what counted as good work, legitimate authority, and appropriate behavior.

Stability Is Practiced, Not Permanent

Routine stability reflects periods when coordination feels natural and predictable. Authority rests in settled interaction patterns rather than active assertion. People move together without renegotiating meaning at every turn. Scripts feel natural because they have been practiced into place.

Yet stability is always a temporary achievement. The same shared meanings that generate order can also produce inefficiency, exclusion, or resistance. Informal status systems may reinforce cohesion while suppressing dissent. Relational harmony may protect morale while limiting adaptation. Stability produces productivity, but it can also conceal fragility.

Small firms inevitably encounter pressures that unsettle these patterns. Crises heighten stakes. Growth stretches identities. When roles shift and resources tighten, the settled understandings that once coordinated work are tested.

Routine stability is the performance through which teams generate order in everyday work. It holds when shared scripts, informal authority, and tacit expectations align around a common understanding of good work. It weakens when new demands strain those scripts beyond what familiar routines can absorb.

Nine Questions to Reveal Your Team's Routine Stability Culture

Most leaders assume culture lives in values statements and mission decks. In practice, it lives in the interaction order of everyday work. During routine stability, shared habits, expectations, and informal power guide coordination long before anyone formally names them.

The questions below are designed to surface those patterned routines and reveal how stability is performed.

See the Pattern: Surface Hidden Routines

1 **What is your organization's ostensive goal—its simple, shared picture of success?**
In everyday language, what do people believe the team is ultimately trying to produce or deliver? Set aside formal mission statements. How does the primary goal actually show up in daily work?

2 **What does "good work" mean in practice?**
Listen to how people praise one another. Is excellence defined by speed, precision, harmony, flexibility, care, or avoiding mistakes? When someone is criticized, what standard are they said to have violated? Whose work is described as "reliable," "strong," or "problematic," and why?

3 **Where does culture show up most clearly in everyday interaction?**
What tensions, risks, or truths surface through jokes or stories? What informal rituals, workarounds, or habits structure the day? How do people signal belonging, or exclusion, in routine moments?

Understand the Stakes: Why Patterns Persist

4 **Which routines feel comfortable even when they limit performance?**
What persists simply because it is familiar? Which practices would feel risky to change, even if improvement is possible? Who benefits most from keeping things as they are?

5 **What problems are safe to raise and which remain hidden?**
What must escalate before it receives attention? Which issues are discussed openly and which circulate in side conversations? When someone raises a concern, how does the group respond?

6 **How does informal power shape everyday decisions?**
Who can bend rules, block change, or redirect priorities without formal authority? Whose opinions carry the most weight when situations are ambiguous? Who is consulted before a decision is finalized, regardless of title?

Shift the Performance: Change Culture in Practice

7 **Where does "that's not my job" prevent better coordination?**
What norms protect boundaries at the expense of teamwork? Which cross-role efforts are supported, and which trigger pushback? When gaps appear, who is assumed to absorb them?

8 **What inefficiencies endure because they protect harmony?**
Where are relationships prioritized over performance? Which recurring frustrations are tolerated to maintain cohesion?

9 **What does the team protect above all else in routine work?**
What reliably provokes correction or escalation? What is repeatedly tolerated, even if it slows progress? What would feel like a violation of "who we are" if changed?

Movement II

Crisis

Chapter 9

Out of Step

Routine Crisis and the Compression of Authority

When work feels calm and predictable, small groups rely on shared values, customs, and expectations that gradually become "how we do things here." What matters, who decides, and what counts as successful work settle into familiar scripts. These patterns allow teams to coordinate and pursue their ostensive goals during periods of relative stability. But calm never lasts forever. Order is always provisional.

Routine crisis performances emerge when the orienting stakes of everyday work sharpen around what must not happen. In these moments, the temporal horizon contracts and the environment intensifies. Settled understandings no longer suffice, and attention narrows to the immediate threat. The emotional tone shifts as well. Fear, urgency, and vigilance rise as teams work to prevent a feared outcome from becoming real. Authority, coordination, and communication reorganize around containment and protecting what feels most vulnerable.

Teams continue pursuing the same ostensive goals, but crises amplify the consequences of failure. Risks feel immediate and unavoidable. As stakes heighten, leaders often assume a more visible role, recalibrating social arrangements and, at times, reducing employee autonomy to contain risk.

In small organizations, these moments are not exceptional disruptions. They recur as recognizable patterns. Over time, teams develop patterned responses. Crisis performances are not invented from scratch. They are negotiated, remembered, and enacted through established interactional histories.

Crisis Is Cultural, Not Universal

Scholars studying organizational crises typically examine two dimensions: decision authority and organizational flexibility under pressure. One line of research, captured in threat-rigidity theory, finds that stress concentrates authority and narrows participation as individuals defer to leadership when stakes rise.[1,2] Other studies find the opposite pattern, showing that

DOI: 10.4324/9781003779803-12

some teams become more cooperative and egalitarian under pressure.[3,4,5] A third perspective suggests both dynamics can coexist, whereby leaders may invite input, but employees remain hesitant to speak up due to norms, uncertainty, or fear of accountability.[6,7,8] Together, this body of work offers insight into how stress reshapes authority and coordination.

Much of this research, however, examines temporary teams or simulated environments where people typically lack shared history. These studies are invaluable for isolating mechanisms under controlled conditions. In ongoing organizations, additional dynamics come into view. Established relationships, norms, customs, and interaction patterns shape how pressure is interpreted and managed. People do not simply revert to formal roles. They respond through trust, experience, and recognizable cultural patterns developed over time. My analysis builds on these insights by examining how crisis unfolds inside small firms with durable relationships and established idiocultures.

If ostensive goals define what good work looks like, routine crisis performances define how that work is protected when failure becomes possible. Under pressure, teams draw on their idiocultures, the localized systems of meaning they have built together. Across the businesses I studied, crises were recognized, interpreted, and managed in markedly different ways, including who spoke, who decided, and how action unfolded. In some settings, leaders centralized control. In others, decision-making became more collaborative. In still others, employees withheld input entirely. These differences reflected each organization's embedded expectations about authority, responsibility, and risk.

Crisis coordination depends on a shared sense of appropriate action, but alignment is rarely automatic. Team members may interpret the same event differently, and responses are worked out through negotiation in real time. Effective crisis performance is therefore not driven by a universal tendency toward collaboration or control. It emerges from the way teams collectively make sense of threat. When sufficient alignment develops, coordinated action becomes possible, grounded in the cultural foundation already in place.

Biggest Fears

Organizational failure is often associated with large, highly complex systems such as nuclear plants, electric power grids, air traffic control systems, and chemical facilities, where breakdowns can produce catastrophic harm. But meaningful risk is not limited to those settings. In small firms, mistakes can also carry serious consequences. At AeroGears, a flawed aerospace component could endanger lives. At ElderCare, a lapse in care could put vulnerable clients at risk. Even in businesses where the physical stakes are lower, such as a florist or a farm, failures threaten reputation, revenue, and long-term business survival. Across all four firms, leaders treated the possibility of failure as consequential, regardless of the objective magnitude of harm.

Each organization had what I came to think of as its "biggest fear," a specific outcome leaders were determined to prevent. These fears were concrete rather than abstract. Leaders referenced them directly when explaining decisions, especially when departing from patterns of routine stability. Over time, employees learned which risks mattered most and how those concerns shaped expectations and priorities. In simple terms, the firms' biggest fears looked like this:

Rolling Hills: A bug in the produce
AeroGears: A plane falling out of the sky
ElderCare: A wandering dementia patient
Thorny Rose: A negative Yelp review

These fears rarely dominated daily conversation. Most of the time, they lingered in the background, a low hum teams grew accustomed to. But when conditions shifted and the risk of failure felt immediate, those fears moved to the foreground. Work took on a different intensity. Employees recalibrated how they performed their ostensive goals. Small behavioral adjustments appeared first. In more serious situations, teams shifted fully into crisis mode, reorganizing coordination to prevent a feared outcome from becoming real.

Stress and crisis are related but distinct. Stress reflects heightened pressure within ongoing operations. Crisis signals the perceived imminence of failure. All organizations operate under some level of everyday risk, but each firm I studied experienced recurring moments when leaders believed a core threat was close to materializing. These moments were unmistakable because the pattern of work shifted. Communication tightened. Authority became more centralized or more assertive. Priorities narrowed. Relationships reorganized around loss prevention. In crisis, the same goal remained. What changed was how urgently it had to be protected.

As perceived risk intensified, routine stability gave way to crisis performances. Employees repositioned themselves, adjusting how they worked together and renegotiating what counted as good work under pressure. Each organization enacted crisis differently, reorganizing leadership, coordination, and responsibility in ways that reflected their underlying cultural logic:

Rolling Hills: Heightened oversight to protect customer trust
AeroGears: Process integrity to prevent catastrophic failure

ElderCare: Centralized authority to protect client safety
Thorny Rose: Directive control to prevent reputational damage

These patterns mirror the range of responses documented in prior crisis research, from concentrated authority to collaborative problem-solving to constrained participation. Yet the variation raises a deeper question: Why do different organizations gravitate toward one response rather than another? The answer lies in culture. Each firm's small group culture shaped how fear was interpreted, how authority was exercised, and how coordination unfolded under pressure.

The next three chapters examine how these crises operated in practice. Chapter 10 pairs Rolling Hills and Thorny Rose, two organizations where crises most often emerge from the pressures of customer expectations. In industries with low switching costs, even small lapses in quality or service can threaten reputation, loyalty, and survival. At both firms, the demand to consistently "get it right" transforms routine work into emotionally charged moments of accountability and conflict. These cases reveal how protecting a brand's promise to customers reshapes internal relationships, decision-making, and the everyday experience of teamwork under strain.

Chapter 11 turns to AeroGears and ElderCare. In these settings, routine work carries serious, sometimes life-or-death, consequences. The line between ordinary operations and crisis is remarkably thin, as precision, compliance, and vigilance define daily life. Yet both teams must balance safety, quality, and financial realities under imperfect conditions. Their stories show how crisis becomes normalized, not as an exceptional rupture but as an ongoing feature of organizational life requiring constant judgment, trust, and emotional resilience.

Finally, Chapter 12 compares crisis performance across cases, highlighting how shared histories, values, and interaction patterns shaped what "effective response" looked like in each setting, sometimes collaboratively, sometimes through tension. Together, these chapters show how crisis unfolds in practice, revealing how teams reorganize work, authority, and relationships as stakes intensify.

Notes

1 Mazzei, Matthew J., Jordan DeBode, Kristin A. Gangloff, and Ruochen Song. "Old Habits Die Hard: A Review and Assessment of the Threat-Rigidity Literature." *Journal of Management* 51, no. 6 (2025): 2154–2181.
2 Staw, Barry M., Lance E. Sandelands, and Jane E. Dutton. "Threat-Rigidity Effects in Organizational Behavior: A Multilevel Analysis." *Administrative Science Quarterly* 26, no. 4 (1981): 501–524.
3 Tajfel, Henri, and John C. Turner. "An Integrative Theory of Intergroup Conflict." In *The Social Psychology of Intergroup Relations*, edited by William G. Austin and Stephen Worchel, 33–47. Monterey, CA: Brooks/Cole, 1979.

4 Willer, Robb. "Groups Reward Individual Sacrifice: The Status Solution to the Collective Action Problem." *American Sociological Review* 74, no. 1 (2009): 23–43.
5 Haslam, S. Alexander, Stephen D. Reicher, and Michael J. Platow. *The New Psychology of Leadership: Identity, Influence and Power*. New York: Psychology Press, 2011.
6 Driskell, James E., and Eduardo Salas. "Group Decision Making under Stress." *Journal of Applied Psychology* 76, no. 3 (1991): 473–478.
7 Detert, James R., and Ethan R. Burris. "Leadership Behavior and Employee Voice: Is the Door Really Open?" *Academy of Management Journal* 50, no. 4 (2007): 869–884.
8 Detert, James R., and Amy C. Edmondson. "Implicit Voice Theories: Taken-for-Granted Rules of Self-Censorship at Work." *Academy of Management Journal* 54, no. 3 (2011): 461–488.

Chapter 10

Reputation on the Line

Rolling Hills

Ostensive goal: Tasty and attractive produce
Biggest fear orienting stake: A bug in the produce
Routine crisis performance: Heightened oversight to protect customer trust

Carrot Boy: Specialization Under Pressure

At Rolling Hills, when the fear of disappointing CSA members intensified, routine stability gave way to a crisis performance marked by tighter oversight and reduced flexibility. On these days, one concern eclipsed all others—making sure no bad produce left the farm.

Although CSA pickup occurred on Tuesdays, much of the harvesting and preparation happened on Mondays. These two days carried higher stakes for Penelope, and her leadership style shifted accordingly. As she often put it, "I don't want a CSA member to get home and a worm crawls out of their salad."

During the rest of the week, Penelope typically asked volunteers about their task preferences and encouraged variety in their work. If a job required less precision, she showed some flexibility about who performed it. But on Mondays and Tuesdays, when timing and quality mattered most, that flexibility disappeared. Penelope assigned tasks directly, prioritizing speed, reliability, and precision over personal preference.

During my first week, Penelope assigned me to carrot collection and sorting. The process was labor-intensive and exacting, requiring careful hoeing, heavy lifting, thorough washing, close inspection for imperfections, and precise bundling. The work often took five hours or more and sometimes carried into the next day. Over time, Penelope noticed that I handled the task efficiently and consistently. What began as a regular assignment evolved into a specialized role. I was eventually asked to train

DOI: 10.4324/9781003779803-13

new volunteers on carrot collection and preparation, and one morning at breakfast Penelope jokingly dubbed me "carrot boy."

Yet even as she relied on me for this critical task, Penelope seemed aware that repeatedly assigning the same person to the same job conflicts with her usual holistic philosophy. Each Monday, she framed the assignment with hesitation:

Penelope: "Eric, I have you down for carrot duty…if that's okay."
Eric: "Sounds good."
Penelope: "I know you've done it a lot already. Do you want to do something else?"
Eric: "I'll look to do something else on another day. Carrots it is."
Penelope: "I want to make sure that you experience other things, but… you're good at it and I don't want to worry about it today."
Eric: "Yes. That works for me. I enjoy…"
Penelope: "Okay, thank you. That's one less thing for me to worry about. Oh, maybe once John finishes the peppers he can help you and you can show him how to bundle the carrots. Does that sound good?"
Eric: "Sounds good."

These extended exchanges were common on Mondays and Tuesdays, when customer pickup loomed. Penelope worked to reconcile two competing logics: her commitment to shared learning and her need for dependable execution. In my field notes, I wrote that I was content with "carrot duty" because I understood how important it was to "get the necessary work of CSA prep done." Other volunteers expressed similar sentiments. Many accepted assignments without complaint, even when they preferred different tasks, because, as one farmhand put it, they did not want to "stress Penelope out any more than she stresses herself out."

Under pressure, variety narrowed into role specialization. Protecting customer trust outweighed holistic development. Practices that felt collaborative during routine weeks took on a more directive tone when stakes intensified.

However, from the volunteers' perspective, these days didn't warrant heightened tension. Most believed the team could harvest, prepare, and set up the CSA pickup space smoothly before members began to arrive at noon without "unnecessary drama," as one fieldhand put it. But Penelope experienced Mondays, and especially "CSA Tuesdays," as moments of heightened risk. Her anticipation of possible breakdowns reshaped her interaction on the farm, tightening oversight, narrowing discretion, and redefining who was entrusted with critical tasks.

The farm's rhythm shifted accordingly. Flexibility gave way to precision. Trust became concentrated in a few proven performers. A normally collaborative, holistic environment took on a more directive, efficiency-driven tone. The ostensive goal remained unchanged, delivering tasty, attractive produce. What shifted was how that goal was enacted when stakes intensified.

4,000 Eggs: When Guidance Feels Like Control

Tuesdays carried an especially pronounce emotional charge. Penelope openly admitted she could "get a little crazy with the CSA," and volunteers felt the shift. Felipe described her as "loco," circling his finger at his temple as he reenacted her yelling, "Filipe! Don't. Don't come in! Don't mess up my floor! I just clean! Stay outside." Similar moments happened whenever workers neared the CSA "showroom," which was simply the home's garage that was transformed each week with foldout tables displaying the harvest produced for members to collect.

Although everyone shared the same goal of delivering high-quality produce, Penelope's leadership intensified under pressure. For volunteers accustomed to holistic, collaborative culture, this shift created tension. Farmhands whispered about her "inability to handle stress," interpreting vigilance as control rather than care.

One incident centered on Damien, a volunteer who had spent three weeks washing eggs and handling lighter farm tasks after a minor back injury prevented him from handling more strenuous labor. Washing eggs required scrubbing residue from shells before packing them into cartons for CSA members. One morning, Penelope approached him while he was at the sink preparing several dozen eggs. With a gentle tone, she said, "Oh, be sure to really clean them good and be sure..." Damien cut her off, raising his voice: "I've cleaned like 4,000 eggs! I know how to do this!" Penelope stiffened, replied "Okay," patted his shoulder, and walked away.

The outburst startled nearby workers. Subtle resistance was common, but open defiance was rare. Later, Damien explained that the instruction felt unnecessary. "She didn't need to tell me what to do," he said. He believed Penelope had been "watching me all morning, like she watches everyone on Tuesdays," which he found "really irritating." Reflecting futher, he admitted, "I was waiting for her to finally say something. When she did, I just got mad." To him, the task was simple: "And it's not like this work is difficult. It's washing eggs!"

Penelope later acknowledged his experience. "He was right," she told me, not about the outburst but about his competence. He had done the task "endlessly in the past," and she admitted she "should not have interfered." Still, she felt she had helpful advice: "I do have suggestions on how he could clean them more quickly. But I don't think he'll listen to me." Beneath her comments was a deeper concern. If quality slipped and CSA members received poorly cleaned eggs, or if not enough eggs were ready when customers arrived for pickup, trust could erode. What Damien experienced as unnecessary oversight, she experienced as risk management.

Stress reframed the interaction. What Penelope intended as guidance felt like micromanagement. Damien, already attuned to the heightened tone of Tuesdays, heard criticism rather than support. From his perspective, the work was under control. Like other volunteers, he did not see Tuesdays as a looming crisis. They were already inspecting produce carefully and ensuring customers received clean, attractive produce.

Penelope's leadership, however, was not uniformly directive. With trusted volunteers like Aiko and Becca, she regularly asked for input on displays and portion sizes for customers, suggesting combinations such as "one large and one small zucchini." These ideas were often adopted, giving those volunteers greater sense of ownership in the CSA operations. Most other farmhands were content to remain in supportive roles. They neither resented not being consulted nor sought greater influence. Their focus stayed on completing assigned tasks well rather than shaping broader decisions.

The tension at Rolling Hills was not about competence or commitment. It was about how leadership shifted under pressure. When stress reframed routine work as crisis, even well-intended guidance felt intrusive. For managers, the lesson is simple: in high-pressure moments, how guidance is delivered matters as much as what is said, especially when teams already feel confident in their roles.

Performing Crisis at Rolling Hills

At Rolling Hills, routine crisis moments, especially Mondays and CSA Tuesdays, triggered a temporary shift in authority. As reputational and logistical stakes intensified, Penelope moved from maternal facilitator to directive overseer, offering closer supervision and more explicit instruction. These days did not signal organizational breakdown, but they did reorganize interactions. Volunteers complied with heightened expectations, even if they did not experience the moment as a genuine emergency. The farm's holistic rhythm endured, but it operated under compressed time and concentrated oversight.

The "4,000 Eggs" episode reveals the limits of this recalibration. When pressure pushed beyond ordinary strain, the calm tone fractured and underlying tensions surfaced. What was usually absorbed through peer coordination became visible as irritation and resistance. Crisis did not overturn the farm's culture. It exposed its fault lines.

At the same time, crisis subtly redistributed influence. Although Penelope often resisted shared decision-making during routine stability, under pressure she selectively sought input from trusted long-term volunteers on matters of presentation and logistics. Authority tightened, yet it also became more strategic. Crisis both centralized control and elevated particular insiders. The result was not cultural transformation but a temporary reconfiguration of power.

Thorny Rose

Ostensive goal: Beautiful arrangements
Biggest fear orienting stake: A negative Yelp review
Routine crisis performance: Directive control to prevent reputational damage

The Meaning of "XX": When Interpretation Breaks Under Pressure

At Thorny Rose, when the threat of reputational harm emerged, the shop's usual diffuse and contentious leadership structure shifted toward more direct and coordinated action aimed at protecting customer trust and containing internal conflict. In these moments, the priority was simple: avoid bad reviews.

Routine business at the florist rested on the assumption that everyone bore responsibility for the shop's success. Leadership was diffuse. Julian managed finances and complex client issues, Nicholas pushed operational speed and employee discipline, and Tyler and Lilia handled design and customer relationships, yet no role was fully contained. Decisions overlapped. Authority was fluid. Any sibling could intervene, redirect, or critique how work was being done. Responsibility was shared, but rarely settled.

This arrangement allowed the family to respond quickly and present a unified front to customers in an industry where, from their perspective, a single negative Yelp review could damage the business's reputation. Whenever a demanding customer emerged, an order went wrong, or someone suggested cutting a corner, Nicholas would declare: "We do whatever we need to do. We don't want a negative Yelp review."

But the system carried costs. Learning occurred through exposure and critique, and critique often slid into personal criticism. Disagreements about how work should be done fueled near-constant arguments. The emotional intensity of these exchanges sometimes drove away non-family and seasonal employees who lacked the shared history to interpret them as normal. Under routine conditions, this fluid authority produced constant friction. Under threat, it became coordinated action.

Yet when real pressure mounted, especially during peak moments like Valentine's Day, the siblings' behavior shifted. As I noted repeatedly in my field notes, they "softened up a bit." Their commitment to customer service did not waiver, but the sharp edges of their internal criticism dulled. Instead of escalating mistakes into arguments, they responded with humor, patience, and collective focus.

This shift became most visible during Valentine's Day, when reputational stakes peaked and even small errors carried significant consequences. That was when I made a mistake that could have jeopardized a customer's personal relationship and harmed the business's reputation.

After several exhausting days preparing for Thorny Rose's busiest and most stressful holiday of the year, I took February 15th off. When I walked into the shop the next morning, Julian stopped me immediately. "Do you remember taking an order for orange tulips on Valentine's Day?" he asked. I did. The customer had been very specific. He wanted a dozen deep-orange tulips with no baby's breath or fillers, delivered to his girlfriend's back porch. Because she lived in a townhouse complex with shared porches, he carefully explained which steps to use and which door was hers. I remembered spending several minutes on the phone making sure I had it right.

Julian told me the customer had called back yesterday. He started the conversation by saying he was very upset. According to Julian, the man said the delivery had almost ruined Valentine's Day and "perhaps damaged their relationship." Still, he apologized in advance if he sounded angry. The customer even complimented me. The person who took his order, he said, was "a really nice and helpful guy." But that same guy had "severely messed up the order."

Julian quickly pulled the paperwork from the stack of nearly a hundred Valentine's Day deliveries. Everything appeared to be in order. The flowers were specified, the colors noted, and the porch directions included. Nothing seemed wrong. Then the customer explained. The card attached to the flowers had a preprinted message at the top: "I love you." The man had only been dating his girlfriend for three months. He hadn't said "I love you" yet.

Julian told me the customer repeated the same line several times: "Hoooooow daaaaaare he." And then followed up with insisting that "He had no right to give that card."

Julian didn't know what happened between the couple that night, but the implication was clear. Explaining that your feelings for someone are strong, but not *that* strong, on Valentine's Day is not an easy conversation. To make things right, Julian offered to send a follow-up bouquet of orange or yellow roses with a balloon that read, "I'm thinking of you." He asked the customer what he would like done. "I'm too upset now to decide," the man replied, "but I'll get back to you."

Julian explained to the customer that the shop had been overwhelmed with orders and that I had likely grabbed the closest card available. The customer said I he didn't want me fired, but he was still "very upset about the whole thing." Julian told him we would keep his name on file and send a replacement bouquet, free of charge, whenever he was ready. After the call, Julian showed me the order form. In the message section, I had written "XX, Alex." That's when it clicked. The customer had explicitly asked me to write "XX." I had assumed it was an affectionate sign-off, shorthand for love. In reality, he wanted "XX" because he didn't want the word "love" on the card.

I apologized to Julian. He laughed. Nearby, El Diablo Blanco arranged flowers and chuckled along. No one was angry. No one lectured me. There was no "lesson learned" speech, the kind that often followed minor missteps during routine weeks. Valentine's pressure altered the response.

My mistake wasn't the only one. Tyler had verbally given a discount to a regular customer. When another customer overheard and asked for the same deal, Tyler refused, and the customer walked out angry. When Tyler told her siblings, they assured her not to worry about it. On a normal day, Nicholas would have scolded her. On Valentine's Day, the rules softened.

This flexibility echoed the shop's everyday approach to learning. At Thorny Rose, both siblings and employees were expected to figure things out by doing them. During routine stability, missed opportunities were tolerated, but critiques were offered, and improvement was assumed. Under peak pressure, however, the priority shifted. Providing feedback and correcting errors mattered less than keeping work moving. Criticism was often softened, deferred, or transformed into humor, preventing frustrations over mistakes from escalating into internal conflict or damaging customer relationships.

Stress didn't just change how work was done. It changed how events were interpreted and how people treated one another. Julian didn't recount my mistake to correct me, but because it was funny. Protecting relationships became as important as protecting revenue.

"XX." No lecture.

"Where Are My Centerpieces?!": A Reputational Crisis

"I'm sorry, ma'am. I do remember you coming in, but I don't see your order." We stood around Julian as he tried to calm a frantic mother on the phone. Her balloon and flower centerpieces for her daughter's Sweet Sixteen hadn't arrived. Guests were expected any minute.

"You have your receipt with you?" Julian asked. "Read it to me and we'll remake the order right now and rush it over."

"Yes, ma'am," Julian continued. "I promise we can make this quickly and beautifully for you. We'll deliver it free of charge, and when you have time to stop by, we'll reimburse you. I do apologize for this." As soon as he hung up, the shop snapped into action. Julian directed Nicholas, Tyler, Junior, the delivery driver, Cody, and me on which balloons to inflate, which flowers to pull, and which van to prep. The order included eight balloon arrangements and three large floral pieces. They weren't complicated, but they needed to be executed quickly and look polished.

Nicholas apologized repeatedly to us as we worked. He had taken the order two weeks earlier and confirmed it the day before, but the order form had never made it into the delivery bin. Julian told the customer there would be slight substitutions, but the color scheme would stay the same. The priority was getting everything there before guests entered the venue.

I found the necessary balloons and ribbons, handing them to Junior who worked the helium tank. Across the shop, Tyler, Nicholas, and Julian assembled the floral pieces, glancing at one another's designs to keep them consistent. Driver Cody cleared the van and pulled up directions. In less than twenty minutes, everything was ready. We loaded the arrangements carefully, and Nicholas and Cody pulled out fast.

As the doors closed, Tyler smiled. "It's amazing how quickly we got that together," she said. "Imagine if we worked that well all the time. We could get so much done." Then she laughed. "But that will never happen."

Thirty minutes later, Nicholas and Cody returned, relieved. The centerpieces were in place, the customer was happy, and Nicholas added that he might have "talked her into giving us a good Yelp review."

The missing order form appeared the next day, clipped to another order by mistake. Nicholas acknowledged he put the two orders together because he thought they were for the same customer. This wasn't unusual. Orders had been misplaced before, deadlines missed, and payments waived to protect the shop's reputation. Systems existed, but Nicholas often relied on memory instead of formal double checks.

Yet in the moment that mattered most, the siblings did not argue or assign blame. They worked. Crisis did not eliminate Thorny Rose's structural weaknesses. It temporarily reorganized them. Diffuse authority became coordinated action. Habitual criticism fell silent. Energy redirected outward toward the customer rather than inward toward one another. The shop's greatest fear, a public reputational wound, was narrowly avoided.

Performing Crisis at Thorny Rose

At Thorny Rose, routine crisis temporarily dissolved the family's usual fragmentation. When the Sweet Sixteen emergency surfaced, shared expertise enabled immediate mobilization. Julian assumed clear authority, assigning tasks rapidly and decisively. No sibling challenged him. No competing instructions emerged. In that moment, hierarchy consolidated. Julian became the unquestioned leader, and the rest of us moved into coordinated support roles. The deference the siblings often expressed privately, acknowledging how much he carried and how much he deserved to lead, was enacted openly and without resistance. For once, the authority they said he merited was fully bestowed.

What makes this episode analytically significant is not simply that the team responded well, but how they responded. Crisis did not produce debate, teasing, or blame. It produced alignment. Despite the shop's everyday pattern of disagreement, no one criticized Nicholas for misplacing the $400 order. Not that day. Not afterward, even when a brief investigation revealed multiple preventable errors. I expected backlash. It never came.

Instead, the siblings reorganized both action and emotion. Frustration gave way to collective responsibility. The immediate stake was reputational survival, not interpersonal scoring. Emotional discipline became as important as technical skill. This alignment allowed the team to resolve the emergency quickly and move through the remainder of the day without reigniting familiar tensions.

But the consolidation was temporary. As soon as the crisis passed, routine hierarchy dissolved back into contestation. Later that day when Tyler left work early rather than finishing the bouquet Julian requested, the old relational dynamics resurfaced. The crisis performance did not resolve underlying tensions. It suspended them.

There was also a structural cost. Although fault was acknowledged, no procedures changed. No safeguards were introduced. Thorny Rose demonstrated remarkable capacity for emotional containment under pressure, yet it struggled to convert crisis into institutional learning. The team could rally. It could repair. It could protect the business. What it could not do was translate crisis into durable structural change.

Chapter 11

When Failure Is Unthinkable

AeroGears

Ostensive goal: A precise part
Biggest fear orienting stake: A plane falling out of the sky
Routine crisis performance: Process integrity to prevent catastrophic failure

"Is There Any Paperwork on This?": Coordination Without a System

At AeroGears, crisis performance centered on protecting precision under pressure. When uncertainty intensified, coordination tightened to prevent technical failure. In these moments, the priority was unmistakable. No failed parts.

Under routine conditions, work followed the simple rule of "stick to your task." Machinists concentrated on cutting metal. Managers focused on keeping jobs moving. For much of the company's history, this loose division seemed sufficient, particularly when the shop handled smaller local orders and repeat commercial work. As Leo recalled, paperwork on jobs once sat in a pile beside his desk. When a machine opened up, they simply grabbed whatever was the next work order. If a customer called with urgency, "We would shuffle through the pile and put their job on top, making their job a priority," he laughed.

Alex described the approach more bluntly. Production happened "from the seat of our pants."

Even after the physical stack of papers disappeared, the logic remained. Scheduling and tracking were largely improvised. Jack carried critical information in his "magical yellow pad," and when customers asked for updates, Alex and Leo had to search the floor to find Jack. Information was concentrated, not systematized. During routine stability, this created inefficiency and frustration. During crisis, it created risk.

DOI: 10.4324/9781003779803-14

In a machine shop, ambiguity is never neutral. Every part produced at AeroGears, whether for a small local customer or a major aerospace client, requires documentation, traceability, and verification. Without records, the shop cannot reliably prove what was made, how it was measured, or whether it met specification. A lapse on a minor job may seem inconsequential, but it reveals the same fragmented coordination processes that govern more critical work. When those same processes touch high-stakes aerospace components, the consequences are magnified. The vulnerability of this arrangement surfaced most clearly in moments when no one could account for a job.

One morning, Jack approached Leo's desk with a customer looking for parts Leo had promised to work on. Leo was not yet at work, and Jack had no idea what the customer was referring to. After searching a cabinet near Leo's desk, he found four loose metal pieces. The customer recognized them immediately. "Those are them," he said.

Jack walked him over to Colleen, the secretary. "This guy wants to give you money," Jack said. Colleen hesitated. "Okay, but I don't know who he is. Is there any paperwork on this?" Jack said there wasn't. The customer mentioned Leo had quoted $315. "It's a one-off job," Jack replied. "Just write something up" Jack said as he walked away. Colleen sighed. "Hold on, hold on... let me find my pad. Geez, you'd think they would have something on this."

I glanced over at Alex, who raised his eyebrows at me, as if to say, "Really? You expected paperwork?"

Colleen wrote up an invoice on a pink receipt pad. The customer paid $315 in cash. While completing the transaction, the customer explained that the parts were for custom microphone stands and that he was a friend of Leo's, perhaps hoping to convey why the work mattered. After the transaction, no records were created. No systems were updated. No one followed up.

The moment captured the larger pattern. Jack didn't know the job existed. Colleen didn't know how to document it. The customer wasn't notified when it was finished. Leo wasn't present for payment and no one bothered to phone him. Everyone stayed in their lane. Work got done, but through informal fixes, limited coordination, and constant low-level strain.

For smaller commercial jobs, this improvisation was inefficient but survivable. But as AeroGears's business shifted toward aerospace contracts, the same coordination habits became more consequential. Informal memory and siloed control were no longer sufficient. Precision now required proof.

Trace Everything: When Formal Systems Increase Pressure

While AeroGears still handled commercial work, its most valuable contracts now came from aerospace clients. General commercial parts allowed the shop greater flexibility in production. As long as tolerances were met, small imperfections rarely mattered. Aerospace parts were different. Precision was nonnegotiable. A small error could be catastrophic. If something failed, AeroGears needed proof that every component met strict standards. Leo remarked at least once a month: "We don't want a plane to fall out of the sky with our parts in it." Precision, in this context, was not just about machining but about documentation.

Aerospace contracts flowed down from major manufacturers like Boeing and demanded flawless records. To qualify as a supplier, AeroGears earned AS9100 certification, an accreditation that governs quality control and traceability. Losing it would end their aerospace business overnight.

Under AS9100 rules, every piece of metal entering the factory arrived with certificates documenting its origin and processing history. Paperwork tracked which machine cut each part, which employee handled it, and how it moved through production. As Alex explained, the goal was to trace every piece "all the way back to the ground it came out of."

For a company built on informal coordination and Jack's "magical yellow pad," this was a profound shift. Alex was initially hired to construct these systems, and the transition was painful. "Getting everyone to understand the importance of accurate documentation," he said, "made me want to shoot myself, or shoot other people. I'd rather go to the beach." Even years later, he still double-checked paperwork others were assigned to complete.

The new standard operating procedures increased work for everyone. Machinists filled out more forms. Managers checked more boxes. Some grumbled that the documentation was repetitive and unnecessary. But no one resisted. The contracts were too valuable. Most machinists told me the added paperwork was "not a big deal." Still, errors persisted. Missing information, incomplete certifications, and documentation mistakes triggered audits, rework, and mounting stress.

The paradox was unavoidable. Systems designed to reduce risk also intensified pressure. Compliance became another layer of strain in an already tense environment. Precision was no longer only about cutting metal. It was about managing paperwork, process integrity, and accountability. And when documentation faltered, the shop faced more than delay. It faced exposure.

That exposure became real during an aerospace contract involving landing gear components destined for military aircraft. What followed was not a machining failure but a documentation breach.

To Rework or Not to Rework?: When "Good Parts" Aren't Good Enough

At AeroGears, crisis did not always begin with a broken part. Sometimes it began with paperwork. The shop's greatest fear was not inefficiency or delay, but exposure: the possibility that a documentation lapse could compromise traceability on parts destined for military aircraft. In aerospace manufacturing, process integrity matters as much as physical precision.

That tension surfaced during a $175,000 contract producing 250 landing gear components for Orland Parts. After machining, the parts were sent to Zenith Metalworks for heat treatment. The order was divided across three purchase orders, each requiring separate AS9100 certificates for traceability. One batch was rejected, returned for minor rework, and sent back under a fourth purchase order.

When the completed shipment returned to AeroGears, three of the four purchase orders arrived in a single box with only three certificate documents. Each batch should have been packaged and documented separately. At first, Alex considered sorting the parts himself. By the next morning, he changed his mind. "That's not the right thing to do," he said. "The right thing to do is to reject the shipment and send it back to Zenith with a new PO."

Internally, AeroGears could trace which machinists cut each piece. But once the batches were mixed, external traceability was compromised. Because all the parts came from the same raw material lot, new certificates could technically be issued. Otherwise, thousands of dollars of finished inventory might have been scrapped.

Jack saw it as a fixable clerical issue. Alex disagreed. They could not use the parts "and simply pretend that nothing's wrong." After discussion, Jack conceded: "You're right. It's an exposure. It should be reworked."

The parts were almost certainly fine. Zenith "does good work and all those pieces are likely good," Alex admitted. His frustration was palpable. "It took me thirty hours to go through the paperwork on this the first time." Still, he insisted, "we shouldn't sweep it under the rug… even though this will put us behind, because it'll take fifty-six days to get this job reworked."

The stakes were explicit. The components were destined for Blackhawks and F-18s. "If something did happen," Alex said, "you don't want to be the one that made that decision."

After contacting Orland Parts, Alex received approval to strip and reprocess the shipment. Further review found shared fault. AeroGears had initially sent three purchase order with only one certificate, and Zenith failed to flag the discrepancy.

Later, Jack reflected on how easily the shipment could have been accepted.

> We machined [these parts] on the same machines… everything was the same… The way that document's written, we could mix them altogether… when the Navy gets them, they just put them all on a shelf. It's all to maintain the integrity of the process.

Alex agreed, saying, "Absolutely. That's all what it's all about."

The debate captured a familiar tension between efficiency and discipline. Jack questioned reworking good parts over paperwork alone. Alex prioritized protecting the "integrity of process" to avoid cutting corners.

The final decision came after Leo returned from a client visit. Alex, who already left work for the day, had joked on his way out the door about the burden of judgment: "It doesn't matter if the job is late or not... So what do I make this decision on? My integrity. It's the right thing to do. I'm Alex and I leave at five. That's my world." Later, he reflected that under pressure people are tempted "to just sweep it under the rug... Yesterday they thought to do this, but a day later they changed their minds. Cool heads prevailed."

Jack and Leo ultimately agreed to rework the parts and share costs with Zenith. The result was delayed delivery, reduced profit, and a compliance mark against AeroGears. But, as Alex noted, the components went into military aircrafts "and served as anti-crash devices... so it mattered."

Performing Crisis at AeroGears

At AeroGears, crisis is not triggered by bad parts alone but by threats to process integrity. Precision extends beyond machining to documentation, traceability, and proof. The ability to track a component "all the way back to the ground it came out of" serves both regulatory and symbolic purposes. It preserves AS9100 certification and signals that the firm is competent, accountable, and deserving of its place in the aerospace supply chain. In this setting, documentation becomes the mechanism through which catastrophic failure is prevented.

During routine operations, Jack governs the shop floor unilaterally. Alex seldom challenges him, and Jack rarely seeks Alex's input. Authority is settled and largely uncontested. But when the documentation breach surfaced, that pattern shifted. Alex raised the concern directly, and Jack invited him into the decision-making process. This exchange was notable precisely because it did not appear in my field notes outside of crisis moments.

The collaboration, however, had boundaries. Alex believed the parts should be reworked, rooted in his position in regulatory compliance and personal integrity. Formally, quality decisions fell within his domain. Informally, final authority still rested with Jack and Leo. Alex pressed the issue carefully, then deferred. Given the company's hierarchy, his restraint was pragmatic. As he often suggested, he preferred to "leave at five" rather than carry the full burden of a high-stakes internal confrontation.

In the end, crisis temporarily widened consultation and loosened the shop's usual lane discipline without redistributing power. The rigid "stick to your task" logic softened as documentation, production, and management briefly converged around a shared threat. AeroGears enacted process discipline to prevent catastrophic exposure, but its hierarchy remained intact. Once the decision was made and the risk contained, roles settled back into their familiar boundaries. Crisis reorganized interaction. It did not reorganize authority.

ElderCare

Ostensive goal: Compassionate care
Biggest fear orienting stake: A wandering dementia patient
Routine crisis performance: Centralized authority to protect client safety

Constant Vigilance: Managing Everyday Risk in Home Health

At ElderCare, crisis did not erupt from a single dramatic event. It emerged when the possibility of client harm became immediate. In those moments, the organization's usual collaborative rhythm narrowed into a centralized performance in which safety overrode consultation. The expectation was unmistakable, ensuring that no harm came to clients.

Unlike Rolling Hills, where pressure peaked around CSA distribution, or Thorny Rose and AeroGears, where crises flared around customer complaints or documentation errors, ElderCare operated under ongoing vulnerability. Risk was not episodic. It was ambient. Nearly two dozen home health aides were scheduled each day to care for elderly clients, and keeping those visits on track required constant coordination. Recruiting and retaining reliable aides was difficult, and Alice and her team routinely managed no-shows, late arrivals, incomplete care plans, and unexpected client needs.

Most days, these disruptions were absorbed through collaboration and improvisation. But each missed visit or delayed arrival carried real consequences for fragile clients. What appeared operational on the surface always contained the potential for harm. Crisis at ElderCare was less about spectacle and more about vigilance. When the risk sharpened, authority consolidated quickly, communication tightened, and decisions were made with little room for debate.

Both Jenn and Alice articulated this fear in blunt terms. Jenn would say, "We don't want a news story about one of our clients who's wandered off into the woods." Alice's version, reflecting her position as the owner, was even more pointed. "I don't need my face on the news saying that we killed somebody." At times, Jenn added another warning: "We don't want some news story with hidden camera footage of our aides hitting an elderly."

Despite this constant concern and the mental strain imposed, the organization functioned effectively. Its routines for staff communication, problem escalation, and decision-making created enough order to keep care delivery on track. The system did not eliminate stress, but it contained it.

At ElderCare, crisis was not an interruption to routine work but an ever-present condition requiring continual monitoring and rapid intervention. What follows are three everyday incidents that illustrate how ElderCare's routine business performance enabled leaders and staff to respond productively, even when things did not go as planned.

Enforcing Compliance Under Pressure

When a home care aide was assigned to fill in for a colleague, Jenn ensured the replacement was thoroughly briefed. The day before the shift, Jenn explained the client's condition to the aide over the phone, emphasizing that he was a fall risk and needed constant supervision. That morning, Jenn followed up with a reminder text as the aide arrived at the client's home.

Later that day, the client's daughter called the office after she checked in on her father. The aide, the daughter reported, was sitting in the kitchen eating while her father remained alone in the adjacent living room. A wall separated the rooms preventing visual supervision. Jenn apologized and assured the daughter that the situation would be addressed. They agreed the aide would finish the shift and Jenn would reiterate the supervision requirement immediately.

After hanging up, Jenn expressed her frustration to the office:

> What?! What part of "Mr. Taylor is a fall risk and you need to be with him all the time" don't you understand! After I spoke about it with you yesterday, you then respond back to a reminder text about it with "OK" and then at 11 o'clock you sit down in the kitchen to eat your soup and sandwich and you can't see Mr. Taylor! I'm going to take a pretty little pill when I'm 80 years old and I'm gone. Because if you leave me with one of these aides, I'm going to hurt them. Or they're going to hurt me!

Jenn called the aide immediately. From her side of the conversation, it was clear the aide was resistant to the expectation, particularly when the client was seated or lying down. Jenn did not debate. When she ended the call, she walked into Alice's office. The conversation was brief. When Jenn returned to her desk, she turned to me and said they felt bad that the client would have a third aide in three days, but the current aide "needs to go."

In routine weeks, ElderCare relied on coaching and collaboration to improve performance. In moments like this, consultation narrowed and authority centralized. Compliance was nonnegotiable when client safety was at risk. Crisis did not invite discussion. It demanded decisive enforcement.

Balancing Care, Family, and the Business

Alice regularly communicated with two daughters of a long-term ElderCare client, even though the sisters often disagreed about their father's care. Over time, Alice became an informal broker between them, coordinating updates and smoothing logistical tensions.

When one sister scaled services back to two hours a day, three days a week—far less than Alice believed appropriate for the client's needs—Alice contacted the other sister to question the change. Alice explained she wasn't sure "if that provided the sort of security she was looking for... so I just wanted to let you know." After the call, Alice told the office the sister responded, "That won't work for me."

We all reacted with humor. Jenn asked, "Are you starting sister fights?" A nurse filing paperwork that day added, "Sisters don't need someone to instigate a fight, they just fight." Jenn chimed in, "Ohhhh, she's going to be mad at you. You told on her!" I suggested Alice was providing the sisters fodder for their next family therapy session. Despite the teasing, the call had its intended effect. The next day, a request for additional hours was placed.

When making the decision, Alice weighed several competing stakes at once. Client safety, family dynamics, business stability, and caregivers' job security all hung in the balance. When hours are reduced, aides often assume they have done something wrong, even when that is usually not the case. Alice preferred stable schedules so caregivers could earn reliable pay and remain committed to ElderCare. Her lighthearted "tattling" achieved several outcomes simultaneously, including better care for the client, reassurance for the family, financial consistency for the provider, and continuity for the business.

At ElderCare, moments like this rarely required formal escalation. They were managed through relational skill, humor, and influence. Stability was sustained not only through policies and protocols but through everyday negotiation. Alice's authority here was not directive. It was persuasive, grounded in trust and shared concern. Through small interventions, she reinforced care standards while preserving cohesion across families, staff, and the business.

"You're Not Mia"—Decisive Leadership When the System Is Tested

What began as a routine scheduling request one day became a high-stakes test. A long-term client needed weekend coverage while their adult children were traveling. The weekday live-in aide was unavailable, so ElderCare scheduled Mia to cover from Friday morning through Sunday night. Because it was Mia's first time in the home, Regina, one of the nurses, was assigned to make the introduction. The current aide on shift, Nicole, was expected to provide in-home training. Everything appeared coordinated until Mia failed to arrive.

At 10:15 a.m., Regina called the office. Mia was already fifteen minutes late. Neither Regina nor Alice could get ahold of her. At 10:30 a.m., Mia texted that she was "on my way." By noon, she still had not arrived. Alice tried calling again. "Of course, now she's not picking up her phone. Who calls saying they're on their way and then two hours later, they're still not there?!" she said.

Soon after, Mia called Alice, claiming she was standing outside the home. Alice asked her to describe it. Alice said, "It sounds like it's the right house." Alice placed Mia on hold and called Regina on the other line. "Mia says she's there standing in the driveway, but you don't see her?" Regina replied, "I'm in the driveway, I don't know what to tell you, she not here." Alice transferred back to Mia, but she had already hung up. Alice stared at the phone. "What the heck is going on?!"

When Mia called again, Alice clarified the street name. Mia was at North Palms. The client lived on North Leaf. The homes looked similar. "Listen, stay right there and I'm coming to get you," Alice said. She hung up with Mia and called Regina. "I can't have [Mia] move and have more of a problem. I'm going to pick her up." Regina hesitated and said, "But now Nicole's shift is over and she wants to leave." Alice didn't waver, saying, "Tell her to take a chill pill. She needs to train Mia for like an hour. Nicole has been there for five months. She can stay for two more hours." Regina responded slowly, "Okaaaaay." Alice left the office.

Twenty-five minutes later, Alice returned with a woman close behind. Jenn asked, "Did you get her?" Alice replied, "Yup, she's right here." Jenn and I exchanged confused looks. Alice sat down and looked at the woman. Calmly, Alice said, "This is illegal. Do you know that?" Then she asked, "Who are you? Because I don't think you're Mia."

The woman insisted she was Mia. Alice asked, "If I call Mia's phone, will it ring in your purse?" The woman said her phone was in her car. Alice asked for ID. The woman said her wallet was in her car. "I know that you're not Mia, so who are you?" The woman finally admitted she was Mia's friend, a nursing student, filling in because Mia could not make the shift.

Alice didn't hesitate. "Do you know how illegal and wrong this is? Okay, get out of my office." As the woman left, Alice added, "And you can tell Mia that I will be reporting her to the Board of Nurses and that she will likely be losing her license."

Afterward, Alice explained that she had suspected something immediately when she drove up to the home. She said she told the woman, "You don't look like Mia. You also don't sound like Mia. I know what Mia looks like. I hired her." When Jenn suggested the woman may not have realized the seriousness of the situation, Alice replied, "It doesn't matter. It's illegal. That's fraud." She sighed. "Now I've got to call the Board of Nurses and report this. She's going to lose her license. Why would she do that and jeopardize her license?" Then added, "At least I knew what [Mia] looks like." When Jenn suggested it probably happened elsewhere in the industry, Alice nodded. "It actually happened here another time."

The risk had been significant. Had the impersonator entered the home, ElderCare could have faced legal liability, reputational damage, regulatory sanction, and potential harm to a vulnerable client.

But one crisis gave way to another. The weekend still needed coverage. Regina remained with the client while Alice and Jenn reworked the schedule. Unable to secure one aide for the full stretch, they divided the weekend into twelve-hour shifts. Alice called Roberta, a relatively new aide who had already shown reliability. "Hi Roberta. I have my next problem." Roberta agreed to the shift. Alice joked, "God bless the child that shows up and is polite. We'll ruin her within six months." Jenn sent additional texts, and together they assembled a team of experienced caregivers to cover the hours needed.

Even then, frustration lingered. "All I can do is find aides to fill the hours," Alice said. Jenn added, "Four different aides in two days for a guy with dementia... That's another client we're screwing around with."

Before the day ended, Alice turned the episode into policy. "From now on, we're going to have every live-in come here first. I will not have them go directly to the home. We will train them here."

What unfolded was crisis leadership in real time. An impersonator was removed. A serious violation was reported. Staffing was rebuilt. A new safeguard was institutionalized. The system bent under pressure but held because authority centralized immediately, consultation narrowed, and client safety remained nonnegotiable.

Performing Crisis at ElderCare

At ElderCare, the crisis carried both practical and reputational stakes. The organization's legitimacy as a trusted home health provider rested on client safety, regulatory compliance, and families' confidence. Whether confronting an aide who ignored fall-risk supervision, brokering disagreements between family members, or removing an imposter from a client's home, leaders acted from a shared understanding that even small lapses could result in serious harm.

The impersonation incident required immediate and sustained attention. Alice spent nearly three hours managing the violation. Jenn devoted roughly an hour coordinating replacements. Regina remained at the client's home for most of the day, leaving ElderCare to absorb the costs of five hours of unplanned labor. Additional weekend staffing was also required to stabilize care.

Less visible costs accumulated as well. While fill-in aides appreciated extra income, most preferred advance notice for weekend shifts. Last-minute appeals risked undermining morale and confidence in the organization's coordination. Jenn framed some requests as personal reciprocity, telling two aides, "I owe you one!" Such favors function as social currency. When spent to contain crisis fallout rather than strengthen the organization's mission, they draw down relational reserves.

What shifted most clearly was Alice's leadership. During routine stability, she favored collaborative and deliberative decision-making. Under crisis conditions, she moved swiftly and unilaterally. She removed the imposter, contacted the licensing board, reassigned staff, and reestablished care continuity with minimal consultation. Authority centralized decisively. Yet this consolidation did not fracture trust. Jenn and Regina aligned quickly, demonstrating that temporary centralization can coexist with a relational culture when stakes are unambiguous.

Unlike at Thorny Rose or AeroGears, ElderCare converted crisis into structural adjustment. Alice immediately instituted a new policy requiring all live-in replacements to report to the office for verification and training before entering a client's home. The change formalized oversight and reduced the likelihood of recurrence. Crisis did not merely reorganize interaction. It strengthened institutional safeguards.

ElderCare's crisis performance therefore reveals a distinctive pattern. Collaboration yields to decisive authority when client safety is threatened, but the underlying relational culture remains intact. Crisis concentrates power without eroding cohesion and produces learning without destabilizing trust.

Chapter 12

The Logic of Crisis

Leading When Everything Is on the Line

When stress rises or a crisis hits, companies do not invent new ways of working. They draw from patterns already embedded in teams. The shared habits, values, histories, and informal rules that guide everyday work also shape how teams respond when something goes wrong.

During routine stability, teams pursue their ostensive goals through familiar coordination patterns. As urgency intensifies, interaction shifts. Authority tightens or redistributes. Communication becomes more direct. Roles narrow or expand. These adjustments culminate in a crisis performance when the responses feel legitimate within the team's existing cultural logic.

Across the four firms, crisis did not produce chaos. It activated patterned responses rooted in each team's idioculture.

At Rolling Hills, Penelope moved from her relational faciliation to directive oversight during CSA preparation days. She assigned critical tasks to trusted volunteers to safeguard quality. Volunteers complied, but because they did not interpret the moment as urgent, authority felt imposed rather than collectively embraced.

At Thorny Rose, sibling tension evaporated when a major order went missing before a Sweet Sixteen party. Julian assumed control without resistance. His long-standing role as family stabilizer seamlessly translated into business leadership. Cultural history, not formal hierarchy, determined who led.

At AeroGears, a traceability breach threatening aerospace compliance temporarily drew Jack and Alex out of their lanes. They reviewed documentation together and debated the appropriate response. Yet when a final decision was needed, authority reconsolidated. Expanded consultation operated within an intact hierarchy.

At ElderCare, an impersonation incident triggered immediate centralization. Alice acted decisively, removing the imposter, stabilizing coverage, and instituting new safeguards. Staff aligned quickly. Because everyday culture emphasized trust and shared responsibility for vulnerable clients, tightened authority felt necessary rather than coercive.

DOI: 10.4324/9781003779803-15

Legitimacy Determines Whether Crisis Performance Holds

Although each crisis unfolded differently, the variation was patterned. Some teams centralized authority. Others broadened collaboration. In some cases, tension intensified. In others, it dissipated. These differences were not random. They reflected shared understandings of what was truly at stake.

A situation becomes a crisis only when members collectively recognize that something important is threatened. At Rolling Hills, Penelope experienced urgency that volunteers did not fully share. That mismatch generated friction. At Thorny Rose and ElderCare, the threat was widely acknowledged. Reputations and client safety were on the line, so decisive authority felt appropriate. At AeroGears, the prospect of compliance failure and aircraft risk elevated the moment enough to justify intensified coordination within an otherwise centralized structure.

Crisis, then, is not merely situational. It is interpretive.

Shared definitions of urgency guided concrete choices. In every case, leaders had alternatives. Penelope could have deferred to volunteers. ElderCare could have declined last-minute coverage requests. Thorny Rose could have let the floral mistakes stand. AeroGears could have advanced imperfect documentation. Instead, each organization selected a response consistent with its cultural logic.

These decisions were practical, but they were also symbolic. They reaffirmed what the company stood for and how responsibility should be exercised during periods of strain. Under pressure, culture did not recede. It structured authority, justified trade-offs, and defined what counted as responsible action.

Crisis performance holds when shifts in authority align with shared meaning. It destabilizes when interpretations of what is at stake diverse. The decisive factor is not the severity of the event, but whether those enacting the response regard it as legitimate.

Routine crisis performance, then, is the patterned reorganization of authority and coordination when stakes rise. It succeeds when cultural interpretations converge. It falters when they fracture.

Nine Questions to Reveal Your Team's Crisis Culture

During routine operations, cultural patterns remain in the background. When orienting stakes rise, they come into sharp view. Teams must decide what counts as unacceptable loss, who has authority to act, and what good work means under strain. Crisis reorganizes meaning, relationships, and decision rights in visible ways. Effective performance is not simply about speed or control. It depends on whether shifts in authority and coordination feel legitimate to those enacting them. Organizations that understand their own rhythms are better equipped for disruption because they share meaning, not just rules.

The questions below help leaders surface the informal scripts that shape coordination when stakes are highest.

See the Pattern: What Really Happens Under Pressure

1 **What does your team treat as a true crisis versus ordinary stress?** Where do leaders feel urgency that employees do not? What outcome does the team organize around preventing? What is their "biggest fear"? At what point does tolerance turn into alarm?

2 **How do people recognize that normal routines no longer apply?** What language, workflow shifts, meeting patterns, or emotional cues signal that crisis mode has begun? Who declares the shift? Who resists it? What behaviors change first?

3 **How does authority reorganize when stakes rise?** Does decision power centralize, move to experts, or narrow to a trusted few? Who gains influence? Who loses it? Which forms of involvement calm the situation, and which consistently generate resistance?

Understand the Stakes: What the Crisis Reveals

4 **What unacceptable loss is everyone trying to prevent?** When that "biggest fear" feels near, what shifts first: oversight, tone, tempo, or control? Which risks receive immediate attention? Which remain in the background?

5 **Who participates in crisis sensemaking, and who disappears?** Is influence concentrated in the formal leader, the most experienced person, the information gatekeeper, or the one others instinctively defer to? Whose expertise suddenly becomes central? Whose input is sidelined? What might change if participation widened?

6 **When trade-offs become unavoidable, which values win?** Does the team prioritize speed, safety, quality, relationships, rules, or visible success? What definition of integrity guides action under pressure? Which values are deferred, diluted, or abandoned?

Shift the Performance: Intervene Without Undermining Legitimacy

7 **How is leadership intervention interpreted under pressure?** Which actions feel like necessary coordination? Which feel like intrusive control? Does tightened authority generate alignment, or does it leave resentment that lingers after the moment passes?

8 **How are mistakes handled during crisis?**
Are errors surfaced for learning, absorbed to keep work moving, or punished to reinforce authority? Does transparency expand or contract? After the crisis, are breakdowns examined openly, or does the team move on without reflection?

9 **Does the crisis leave a scar, a lesson, or nothing at all?**
When pressure subsides, what changes endure? Are safeguards introduced, policies revised, and responsibilities clarified? Or does the organization revert to familiar patterns? What transforms disruption into institutional learning rather than temporary survival?

Movement III

Growth

Chapter 13

Learning New Steps

Routine Growth and the Recasting of Identity

Organizations rarely sit still. Even during ordinary work, people are constantly coordinating, adjusting roles, and making real-time decisions to keep activity aligned. In crisis, pressure sharpens around what must not happen. Fear reorganizes authority, tightens coordination, and temporarily clarifies priorities. Growth operates through the same structural mechanism, but with a different emotional logic. Instead of guarding against loss, orienting stakes shift toward what the organization believes it must become. Where crisis heightens fear, growth heightens aspiration, and aspiration is harder to align.

Routine growth performances emerge when anticipated opportunity expands the horizon of action. While ostensive goals define what good work looks like, routine growth reshapes how that work is extended, scaled, and reinterpreted. Uncertainty is no longer something to contain. It becomes something to pursue. As this shift occurs, established patterns loosen. Roles evolve. Authority is renegotiated. Coordination is reconfigured in pursuit of expansion and legitimacy. These adjustments rarely unfold according to formal plans. Growth strategies may be articulated at the top, but they are enacted locally through everyday interaction.

Unlike crisis, growth does not automatically unify a team around a shared threat. It requires members to reinterpret who they are, what success means, and whose priorities will guide expansion. Stability preserves identity. Crisis protects it. Growth unsettles it.

For this reason, growth is often the most fragile of the three performances. It demands change without the clarity of danger. It disrupts routines without the urgency of survival. And because opportunity is interpreted differently across members, growth can expose fault lines that stability and crisis temporarily conceal.

Growth and the Unsettling of Group Relations

Any shift in conditions destabilizes the unwritten agreements that hold a team together. The shared meanings, habits, and expectations that once

DOI: 10.4324/9781003779803-17

made work coherent no longer fully fit emerging demands. Adjusting tasks is easier than reworking meaning. When members no longer understand why work is being done differently, or what those changes imply about who they are as a group, coordination begins to fray.

In many organizations, growth conversations happen primarily at the top. Strategic plans are drafted by senior leaders and handed downward. But when the rationale for expansion, the risks involved, and the implications for daily work are not collectively interpreted at the team level, change feels imposed rather than owned. Compliance may follow, but commitment often does not.

Group cultures evolve through shared experience. Identity is built through repeated routines and daily interaction. When growth reshapes roles, valued skills, or definitions of competence, those identities are unsettled. Authority can mandate new procedures, but it cannot manufacture shared purpose. It cannot assume that members possess the repertoire, or the desire, to enact a new future.

As identity coherence weakens, cohesion erodes. Sometimes this happens quietly, through disengagement and withdrawal. Sometimes it surfaces as open resistance, conflict, or exit. Growth is not merely operational expansion. It is cultural reorganization. And without shared meaning, expansion destabilizes the very coordination it depends upon.

Meaning Management, Social Skill, and Institutional Entrepreneurship

If growth destabilizes meaning, leadership during expansion requires more than authority. It requires the capacity to reshape shared understanding. Sociologist Neil Fligstein describes this capacity as social skill, the ability to induce cooperation by framing situations in ways that resonate with others' identities and interests.[1,2] In unsettled moments, socially skilled actors redefine priorities, establish new interaction patterns, and position change as legitimate rather than imposed. Sociologist Paul DiMaggio refers to those who effectively mobilize other around new visions as institutional entrepreneurs, actors who transform organizing principles by reconstructing meaning.[3]

Across the firms in this book, leaders often relied more on directive authority than on social skills to advance growth. Work moved forward, but share understanding did not always keep pace. Informal challengers emerged, not as competitors for formal power but as defenders of established identities. By questioning motives, emphasizing trade-offs, and protecting valued routines, they influenced how expansion unfolded in practice.

Growth did not stall. It proceeded. But without sufficient meaning alignment, coordination slowed, morale declined, and relationships frayed. Expansion advanced operationally, while cultural cohesion weakened. Growth, in these cases, was achieved, but not fully integrated.

Growth Orienting Stakes

When organizations pursue growth, they reorder what feels most important in everyday work. Growth is not simply an increase in volume. Orienting stakes heighten attention to opportunity, reputation, and momentum, reshaping how time is allocated, how roles expand, and how much strain the team is willing to tolerate.

Unlike crisis, where stakes center on preventing loss, growth stakes center on becoming. They elevate an imagined future and organize present action around it.

Across the firms I investigated, expansion introduced identity-level tensions about what the organization was becoming and what could be lost along the way. Leaders anchored growth in recognizable images of industry success, using those models as orienting stakes to define what "real growth" should look like. These stakes carried both aspiration and risk. Teams were not only pursuing revenue or contracts, but they were navigating questions of legitimacy, capacity, quality, and control. The day-to-day version of each stake sounded like this:

Rolling Hills: Evolve into a full-service farm
ElderCare: Become the region's go-to home health provider
AeroGears: Transform from a job shop to a world-class manufacturer
Thorny Rose: 1. Preserve exceptional customer service; 2. Grow into a premier large-scale and event-driven brand

These stakes defined what leaders believed the firm needed to become. Naming that future did not ensure agreement about how to reach it.

Routine Growth Performance

As new opportunities emerged, teams reorganized authority, adjusted coordination, and redefined what counted as competent action. Growth altered tempo, stretched routines, and redefined roles. Yet each firm enacted a patterned growth performance shaped by its existing idioculture.

Rolling Hills: Diversification of offerings to deepen customer relationships
ElderCare: Active client acquisition paired with intensified staffing coordination

AeroGears: Output-driven production and continuous shipping
Thorny Rose: 1. Always-on responsiveness to customers; 2. Strategic prioritization of high-revenue projects

As with crisis, the ostensive goal remained constant. What changed was how teams enacted it under new orienting stakes. These performances embodied ambition, but they did not guarantee the relational or structural capacity required to sustain expansion. Existing coordination patterns were stretched beyond their original design. Strain accumulated. Authority realigned as expectations intensified. Meaning-making grew contested.

In each firm, growth raised the same underlying question: How do we expand without losing what makes us who we are? At Rolling Hills, diversification strained the informal social contract. At ElderCare, growth shifted attention from relational oversight to logistical coordination. At AeroGears, growth often outpaced the systems needed to support it. At Thorny Rose, competing visions of growth turned expansion into a struggle over coordination, authority, and identity.

Growth did not unfold as smooth adaptations. The orienting stake generated pressure. The consequences were uneven, sometimes productive, sometimes destabilizing.

Taken together, these cases show that growth is not linear operational expansion. It is a cultural performance through which teams reshape authority, tempo, and definitions of good work. Stability preserves order. Crisis compresses coordination around threat. Growth expands possibility and, in doing so, unsettles the identities that once made coordination effortless. How expansion unfolds depends on what the group believes is at stake and whether it can renegotiate meaning without eroding cohesion.

The next three chapters examine what happens when organizations move beyond routine stability and crisis in pursuit of growth. Expansion tests existing arrangements, redistributes authority, and creates opportunities for institutional entrepreneurs to influence the direction of change. The performances that emerge are not predetermined. They reflect how teams respond when familiar routines can no longer sustain emerging ambitions.

Chapter 14 follows Rolling Hills and ElderCare as they diversify, only to discover that expansion reshapes identity, workflow, and moral boundaries in ways employees often resist. Chapter 15 turns to Thorny Rose and AeroGears, where the pursuit of higher output and industry legitimacy exposes clashing values, fragile coordination, and mounting confusion. Across all four firms, ambition unsettled the shared understanding that once anchored teamwork.

Chapter 16 draws broader lessons from these cases, demonstrating that growth driven primarily by top-down decisions and limited opportunities for collective interpretation leaves employees disoriented at precisely the moment when alignment is most critical. Sustainable expansion requires inclusive sensemaking, transparent articulation of purpose, and deliberate protection of trust as teams navigate shifting organizational rhythms.

Notes

1 Fligstein, Neil. "Social Skill and Institutional Theory." *American Behavioral Scientist* 40, no. 4 (1997): 397–405.
2 Fligstein, Neil. "Social Skill and the Theory of Fields." *Sociological Theory* 19, no. 2 (2001): 105–125.
3 DiMaggio, Paul. "Interest and Agency in Institutional Theory." In *Institutional Patterns and Organizations*, edited by Lynne Zucker, 3–22. Cambridge, MA: Ballinger, 1988.

Chapter 14

Rewriting Roles

Rolling Hills

Ostensive goal: Tasty and attractive produce
Growth orienting stake: Evolve into a full-service farm
Routine growth performance: Diversification of offerings to deepen customer relationships

Expanding the Farm, Stretching the Team

At Rolling Hills, routine growth centered on becoming a full-service farm by expanding beyond production. New revenue streams were layered onto everyday work, often without fully redefining what volunteer labor should include. Growth broadened everyone's responsibilities without explicitly redefining what volunteer labor entailed, producing subtle fractures in trust and belonging.

Because Rolling Hills depends primarily on its CSA membership for revenue, one path to growth would have been expanding membership. But the local market was crowded. Although membership had increased steadily, Penelope does minimal marketing. New customers arrive entirely through word of mouth. She describes neighboring CSA farms as run by "young couples with lots of energy" who have successfully "create[d] a community of members" through educational events, shared meals, discussion groups, and cooking classes. These farms offer not just produce but a social experience.

Penelope sees the appeal but knows she cannot compete on those terms. While she considers herself "much better than most people my age," she lacks the energy to host regular community events. Her time is already divided among farm operations, guest lectures at schools on the Rudolf Steiner philosophy of education, and weekly choir rehearsals and performances. Although she values a holistic, community-centered farm culture, she recognizes that this model is not sustainable for her.

DOI: 10.4324/9781003779803-18

Instead, she pursued growth by expanding what she could offer existing customers. She relied on loyal members to "spread the word" while she was developing homemade organic sauces and mixes for sale, rented upstairs rooms to short-term guests with add-on meal options, and sought donor support. Her strategy emphasized diversification rather than outreach. As she told me, "We can do more for our CSA members, sell prepared sauces, milk...." In this way, she believed, "We can compete with those young couples who are first-time farmers."

With limited labor, Penelope drove most of this expansion herself. Volunteers already worked full days under the farm's informal exchange of housing and food for labor. When growth activities spilled beyond routine agricultural tasks, however, tensions surfaced. Requests for extra help tested the boundaries of what counted as appropriate responsibility. Without a shared redefinition of the farm's work, diversification began to feel less like collective evolution and more like individual extension, revealing how growth can strain a culture built on reciprocity.

Don't Mess Up My Kitchen: Growth and Exclusion in Prepared Foods

Imperfect vegetables that were not "beautiful enough" for CSA members were usually set aside for volunteers to eat. When harvests exceeded what CSA members, restaurants, and volunteers could consume, Penelope saw an opportunity. Drawing on her cooking skills, she decided to transform leftovers into tomato sauce, carrot-ginger soup, pesto, pumpkin purée, and pickled vegetables. To sell these products as certified organic, she quickly built a small commercial kitchen in the garage where CSA pickups took place. Construction and certification moved swiftly. The growth initiative was decisive and largely self-directed.

Once the kitchen was officially ready, however, volunteers were barred from using it. They were told not to wash hands or vegetables there, not to use the refrigerator, and not to touch the stove or oven. Although the space was not essential for daily farm labor, the restriction carried symbolic weight. As one farmhand put it, "we couldn't be trusted not to mess up her precious kitchen." What had been imagined as a shared farm suddenly contained a protected zone.

For many volunteers, the rule clashed with Penelope's earlier framing of Rolling Hills as a holistic place of learning. The kitchen could have been a site for developing new skills, including food preservation, organic certification standards, and small batch production. Instead, it became "off-limits." The boundary regulated behavior and, in doing so, redefined who growth was meant to serve.

Penelope justified the decision in terms of food safety. Proper canning procedures were critical, she explained. Volunteers pushed back, noting that they were willing to learn and that "friends at other farms do those things." Still, Penelope insisted that involving others would slow production. "It would just take forever to get any of this done," she told me.

What volunteers experienced was not simply a new rule but a shift in leadership style. The expansion of prepared foods introduced a more protective, controlling stance, one that communicated explicitly, "stay out of my kitchen." Instead of inviting wider participation, growth narrowed influence and centralized control. Rather than strengthening collaboration around diversification, the new venture sharpened hierarchy and deepened feelings of exclusion. In pursuing expansion, Penelope altered the relational contract that had long sustained volunteer commitment.

Room for Rent: Growth Without Renegotiating the Social Contract

"Pretend Like You're Not Here": Hiding Volunteers to Sell the Farm

Another growth strategy at Rolling Hills involved renting three upstairs rooms in Penelope's house. Guests were primarily visiting faculty working at the local college and short-term travelers staying anywhere from a few nights to several weeks. Amenities were simple, but Penelope viewed higher occupancy as essential, explaining that the extra income could fund livestock she "desperately wanted."

For volunteers, however, the expansion blurred the boundaries between home, work, and belonging. The recruitment process often ignored the fact that farmhands lived communally in the same space. When prospective renters toured the house, Penelope instructed them to "hide your stuff in the closets" and clean up "so it doesn't look like you're here." Cleaning was not an issue for volunteers. Pretending they were invisible was. As Aiko observed, "we still all live in the living room, so it's not like they're not going to figure that out."

The request communicated more than tidiness. It suggested that volunteers were part of the farm's labor system but not part of the image being sold. Growth depended on presenting a polished, orderly household, even if that meant temporarily erasing the people who sustained it.

Some farmhands believed Penelope simply did not recognize the emotional impact of her decisions. One described her as having "some sort of block" when it came to others' feelings. Aiko recalled raising her discomfort directly. Penelope responded with "Ohhhhhhhh," a familiar sound volunteers understood as acknowledgment without adjustment.

As room rentals became more financially important, tensions deepened. What Penelope framed as keeping a "perfectly clean" home increasingly felt like control rather than care. Growth had not been openly renegotiated. It was layered onto existing arrangements, widening the gap between the farm's communal ideals and its daily practice.

"Another Mouth the Feed": When Growth Becomes Emotional Labor

Alongside room rentals, Penelope offered home-cooked meals for $20 per day, usually prepared from farm produce. Although she said she handled the cooking herself, she often relied on Aiko, one of the strongest fieldhands and most capable cooks. Farmhands cooking for one another was expected. Cooking for paying guests was not.

One afternoon, Aiko mentioned a new renter who had arrived several days earlier. When I asked his name, she said she hadn't been introduced. "Penelope keeps forgetting his name," she explained. "Filipe can't pronounce it, so he just calls him 'Young Man.'" She knew only that he was a visiting professor. Then she added, flatly, "It's another mouth to feed."

Laughing, I asked why she framed him like a child. "Because I've been doing all the cooking," she replied. When I suggested someone else help cook, Aiko said, "Nooooo. It's fine. But I'm tired of my own food."

Aiko was preparing extra portions so the renter would "get his money's worth." Other volunteers refused to cook for him. "It's not my responsibility," one said. Another added, "If Penelope wants renters, she needs to take care of them. I'm not working in a bed and breakfast here."

Penelope offered Aiko $10 per day as "play money for when she goes into the city." Aiko felt uneasy accepting it, saying she "felt bad" taking money from someone who was "always talking about how she has so little." Later, Penelope gave Aiko $100, which she accepted reluctantly, "I didn't want to get into a fight...and I wanted to eat out at this restaurant I read about."

The meal plan did not foster a shared investment in growth. It shifted labor and an emotional burden onto one volunteer. Financial incentives unsettled the informal exchange of labor without making the arrangement feel fair. Penelope relied on Aiko's goodwill. Others withdrew. Gradually, farmhands began to see Penelope less as a nurturing "mother-leader" and more as someone advancing personal goals.

After a few weeks, "Young Man" dropped the meal plan. Penelope was "really relieved," Aiko told me. He hadn't liked the food much and thought there were "too many vegetables."

"Is This a Birthday Party or a Fundraiser?": Using Relationships to Mobilize Support

Toward the end of my fieldwork, Penelope began planning a 75th birthday party for her husband, Ross. The invitation she showed me looked both celebratory and strategic. Dinner details appeared at the top. At the bottom, guests were encouraged to make "$25 contributions" toward solar panels. As she explained, "I didn't just want to make it a party. If people are planning on getting Ross a birthday gift anyway, they should help get something he needs." I was fairly certain this was something Penelope, rather than Ross, "needs."

Penelope seemed slightly uneasy about blending a personal milestone with a financial appeal, yet the invitations were already printed. I chose to be encouraging and said it "makes sense to pair efforts to get a solar panel with the birthday," she laughed, saying, "You know I'd wish everyone would come and slap down $75 on the table, but...." Then she asked me to help spread the word among the farmhands so "we can get as many people here as possible." She would need their labor for cooking and serving, tasks that fell outside the formal volunteer exchange.

Because I was well liked on the farm at that point, Penelope positioned me as a bridge to volunteers who might resist. Even as I sensed the "weirdness" of a fundraiser-birthday hybrid, I found myself describing it to others as "important for the farm to continue to grow and be self-sustaining." I had absorbed her framing. As she had with Aiko, Penelope leveraged our personal relationship and my social positioning to mobilize support for growth.

Performing Growth at Rolling Hills

In pursuing her goal of becoming a full-service farm, Penelope attempted to redefine both the meaning of everyday work and the identity of her volunteers. Unlike her usual emphasis on holistic, shared labor, her growth initiatives often excluded farmhands from key decisions while still relying on their goodwill to carry them out. Revenue-generating activities made her financial pressures more visible, yet she rarely connected these efforts to the farm's broader mission. Instead, she relied on direct authority when possible, demanding spotless living quarters and restricting access to the new organic kitchen. Yet she struggled to secure voluntary support for cooking, hosting, and fundraising.

Most volunteers saw themselves as farmhands committed to agricultural and personal learning, not hospitality staff or fundraisers. Even small financial incentives for farmhands failed to shift that self-understanding. Because growth was not framed in terms that aligned with their identity, many volunteers doubled down on their original vision of Rolling Hills as a place for hands-on, communal work.

Penelope did manage to mobilize support through personal relationships. Aiko cooked for renters, and I acted as a broker to encourage participation in Ross's birthday-fundraiser. Over time, some of us internalized the logic that these efforts were necessary for the farm's survival. Compliance followed, but resentment lingered. Short-term gains came through informal influence and selective loyalty rather than genuine collective commitment.

Aiko, whom Penelope had hoped would stay and support future expansion, ultimately left the farm. Her departure revealed the limits of this growth strategy. When expansion reshapes responsibilities without renegotiating meaning, it may generate immediate revenue, but it erodes the trust and shared purpose that sustain collective work over time.

ElderCare

Ostensive goal: Compassionate care
Growth orienting stake: Become the region's go-to home health provider
Routine growth performance: Active client acquisition paired with intensified staffing coordination

No Time to Grieve: When Compassion Meets Revenue Pressure

At ElderCare, routine growth centered on becoming the go-to provider by expanding reach and filling more shifts. This involved taking on more clients as staffing constraints tightened and care standards became harder to maintain. The drive for legitimacy and steady revenue subtly reweighted decision-making toward volume, challenging the balance between compassionate care and organizational survival.

Although compassionate care remained the stated goal, Alice and Jenn quickly learned that the business required emotional recalibration. When their first client died, they cried together and briefly wondered if the work was "too emotionally taxing." Over time, that response changed. In one staff meeting, Jenn explained that when a patient dies, her first thought is now, "Come on people, we need to find some new clients, we need to pick up business." The part-time nurse added that this mindset actually begins "when a patient goes on hospice." Alice confirmed, "That's right."

Alice regularly reminded the team that turnover was structural, not personal. "Thirty percent of business is always in flux," she said. "Many of your clients will die. And you always need to find new clients." Clients routinely passed away, moved into assisted living, relocated, or switched providers. "We need to be on the top of the referral list...we need to be able to fulfill client requests and we cannot turn down opportunities."

Alice tracked revenue on the conference room whiteboard. Breaking even required weekly revenue of $25,000. Many weeks while I worked there, revenue hovered around $18,000. Alice felt that fanchise headquarters were effective at supporting start-ups and large operators but were "not so good with the in-between."

To replace lost clients, ElderCare leaned heavily on referral relationships. Alice hired a salesperson to cultivate hospital and care-facility case managers who controlled access to new business. Competitors moved faster and had deeper staffing pools. Under this pressure, ElderCare's routines shifted. Rather than carefully selecting clients aligned with their care philosophy, the team increasingly adopted a "take all clients" posture. Growth became less about serving the right patients and more about finding clients and keeping shifts filled. Compassion remained the ideal. Capacity utilization became the organizing constraints.

Murky Waters: Taking on Risk to Sustain Growth

"Why Do You Want This Case So Bad?"

Alice frequently voiced frustration about ElderCare's inability to reach stable break-even numbers. "Making $12,500 a week is a failing business," she said. "And when I get up to $17,500, I lose a client. So where does that leave me? I don't know how to get over that hump because we keep slipping back down."

In a conversation I listened in on with her accountant, Alice reflected on the slow path to stability:

Alice: "They [headquarters] tell you it's a two- to three-year thing, but it's really a five-year process...And now we're finally doing okay, but there's always more to be done."
Accountant: "I understand. I see this with a lot of clients."
Alice: "And when do I reach that magic moment..."
Accountant: "...and breathe."
Alice: "If ever, right!"

Under mounting pressure, Alice increasingly prioritized securing clients over quality care matches. During routine operations, staff carefully discussed assignments together. When growth became the priority, speed replaced collaboration. Saying yes became a strategic necessity, essential to becoming a "legitimate" provider and staying visible to hospital case managers who controlled referrals.

Live-in cases were especially valuable. Even without ideal aides available, Alice accepted the cases, framing the risk as necessary for growth.

One morning, Alice assigned an aide named Candice to a three-day overnight shift, despite Candice having recently been removed from another home for ignoring a care plan developed by the nurse. When Jenn returned from lunch, Alice started cautiously. "You're not necessarily going to like what I decided to do, but..." Jenn interrupted, knowing already what Alice decided. "That's a bad idea. Why do you want this case so bad?" Alice pushed back. "We are not building. We are stuck. Look at that wall..." She pointed to the whiteboard listing pending and ending cases.

In another staffing conversation about an aide named Stephanie, who performed inconsistently:

Jenn: "Stephanie is a scuzzball. She would sell her mother for a quarter if she could."

Alice: "Stephanie's free."

Jenn: "I would rather gouge my eyes out than give her more hours."

Alice: "Jenn, we don't want to go down that path. We don't have anyone else if we get those cases."

Jenn: "I know, and I would do it, but it doesn't make me feel warm and fuzzy at night...And just for the record, I'll say it again, Stephanie is a scuzzball."

As introduced in Chapter 4, Alice and Jenn often approached decisions through different interpretive logics. Alice operated with what I earlier described as a shades-of-gray logic, believing imperfect aides were preferable to turning down revenue. Jenn held a black-and-white stance, arguing that poor matches compromised ElderCare's mission. Under routine conditions, these perspectives balanced one another. Under growth pressure, however, the gray logic increasingly prevailed. The collaborative routines that once structured decision-making gave way to faster, risk-tolerant calls. The organization preserved its values, but reinterpreted them to survive.

Do You Even Know Your Aides?

During a Tuesday meeting with ElderCare's part-time consultant, held while Alice was away, Jenn remarked, "We're placing aides that Alice never met before." Jenn explained that Alice now said, "If they have all their paperwork and they have a car, hire them. She used to sit down with every new aide." The consultant responded, "I don't blame her because you need to grow." But then he paused. "That's bad though...she should know better."

Jenn was unsettled by the shift. Where Alice once personally interviewed every caregiver—developing a firsthand understanding of her hires and the ability to spot potential crises, as in the "You're Not Mia" incident—she now focused on eligibility and logistics. Delegation itself was not the issue. What changed was relational oversight. As hiring accelerated, familiarity gave way to throughput.

The consultant framed this as necessary evolution. Alice, he argued, needed to act "like a leader of a large organization" and step away from "daily work that others can handle." Growth required role differentiation. Still, he conceded she should at least meet new hires.

As ElderCare expanded, decision authority dispersed without a fully articulated system to replace it. Jenn absorbed new responsibilities but without the shared grounding that had once anchored staffing decisions. What looked like professionalization to the consultant felt like distance to the team.

"Shuttling Aides Around": When Growth Distorts Roles

Finding reliable aides with their own transportation had been difficult since ElderCare's founding. Public transit was "a nightmare," making it difficult for caregivers to reach clients reliably. During a surge in new clients, Alice hired caregivers without cars, forcing the company to rely on Ubers or taxis that cost hundreds of dollars per week. To cut expenses, Alice began driving some aides herself. Soon Jenn, the nurse, and even I were driving aides as well.

"Jenn has to leave the office and drive people, I have to drive people," Alice explained, "and if we don't, I can't afford to spend like $500 a week on transportation." Jenn pushed back. "Who the hell tells an employee that if they can't get to work, the boss will give you a ride? I've never heard of this! It's ridiculous!"

The arrangement quickly strained the team. Alice missed meetings because she was shuttling aides. The consultant urged her to "stop doing that" and focus on recruiting. After long drives, Alice returned to the office exhausted and avoided problems. As one colleague joked, when Alice was tired she didn't just "bark" at everyone, "she shrieked!" The humor masked real frustration.

Time meant for care coordination and leadership was diverted to logistics. Jenn argued that chauffeuring aides was not part of their professional role. The consultant noted privately that Uber and taxi costs were preferable to damaging morale. The nurse added she "didn't need 20 years of nursing experience to drive people to work."

Eventually, Jenn tracked the time and expense associated with Alice, Jenn, and other staff members providing transportation to demonstrate the practice's hidden cost. Within a month, the office stopped transporting caregivers and Alice sharply reduced her own driving. Through this move, Jenn reinforced the team's core understanding that their work centered on coordinating care rather than absorbing the consequences of growth shortcuts.

Performing Growth at ElderCare

At ElderCare, growth did not begin with new systems or expanded infrastructure. It began with pressure. Under the orienting stake of becoming the region's go-to home health provider, Alice reorganized priorities around accepting clients quickly, filling cases with whoever was available, and protecting revenue streams that were constantly eroding through turnover. Transportation, availability, and speed increasingly outweighed ideal skill fit. Survival logic began to compete with care logic.

These shifts did not eliminate the company's commitment to compassionate care, but they changed how that commitment was practiced. Routine stability had depended on collaborative deliberation between Alice and Jenn. Growth compressed time and narrowed space for shared decision-making. Alice centralized calls and framed compromises as necessary for viability yet struggled to build collective agreement around those trade-offs. Expansion required not only more clients but a recalibration of what compassionate care looked like under financial constraint.

Jenn's resistance was not simply interpersonal tension. It reflected a deeper concern about what the organization was becoming. As staffing shortcuts and cost-driven adjustments accumulated, employees felt the strain between safeguarding vulnerable clients and safeguarding margins. Growth unsettled not just routines but the boundaries of professional responsibility.

ElderCare's growth performance illustrates a common pattern in mission-driven firms. When expansion collides with identity, the central questions become: Which decision rules will prevail. What trade-offs are acceptable? What risks are tolerable? Growth does not automatically erode culture. Without explicit alignment between financial survival and shared purpose, however, it can gradually redefine the relationship between them.

Chapter 15

When Growth Outruns Systems

Thorny Rose

Ostensive goal: Beautiful arrangements
Growth orienting stake: 1. Preserve exceptional customer service; 2. Grow into a premier large-scale and event-driven brand
Routine growth performance: 1. Always-on responsiveness to customers; 2. Strategic prioritization of high-revenue projects

Competing Visions of Growth

At Thorny Rose, routine growth centered on becoming a scaled brand while preserving its identity as a hands-on, service-driven shop. The family sought larger contracts and higher visibility, yet remained deeply attached to craft and personal service. Growth did not simply introduce operational strain; it exposed a fault line in leadership.

Unlike the other firms, Thorny Rose did not have a single, consolidated voice directing expansion. Authority was diffuse, responsibilities overlapped, and no sibling held clear decision-making power. Leadership was both collaborative and contentious, shaped as much by family history and emotion as by formal roles. As a result, expansion became a negotiation over identity, legacy, and whose definition of success would guide the firm.

Thorny Rose therefore developed not one orienting stake for growth, but two. Julian and Nicholas each advanced a distinct vision of what scaling should mean, rooted in their roles and interpretations of the company's legacy. Because orienting stakes shape everyday decisions, these competing visions produced two different growth performances that pulled the organization in divergent directions.

For Julian, growth meant deepening the shop's commitment to constant availability and emotionally attentive service. "Our business is all customer service," he often said. "That's what we offer here." To compete with traditional florists and rivals such as supermarket flower counters, Trader

DOI: 10.4324/9781003779803-19

Joe's, Whole Foods, and even gas stations, he believed Thorny Rose should double down on responsiveness. Beautiful arrangements were important, but what truly differentiated the store, in his view, was doing whatever it took to serve customers well.

If all the siblings shared responsibility for every task, the shop could remain flexible and highly responsive as it expanded. While service was already strong, Julian wanted everyone to take on more in order to reinforce that identity. He was fond of saying, "If a customer buys one rose today, you might wind up doing their $30,000 wedding down the road."

Julian grounded this philosophy in the store's history. Since his grandfather opened Thorny Rose, the shop had almost never closed, except for the funerals of their grandfather and father. Even then, it remained open in the morning of his father's funeral. For Julian, long hours, seven-day operations, and staying open on holidays were not optional but required. Because flower purchases were often spontaneous and emotionally driven, he believed customers expected the shop to be open whenever they stopped by.

Nicholas, however, interpreted both the past and the future very differently. "I don't want to be here every day from morning 'til night," he argued. "What's the big picture here? We should use this place's potential and figure out all the things we can sell." Lilia reinforced this reframing of the family legacy, suggesting their grandfather worked nonstop because "that's what all new business owners need to do," and Nicholas added that their father did it "because he was selfish and wanted money." Rather than replicating that model in the current generation, they envisioned a business that allowed greater balance between work and personal life.

For Nicholas and Lilia, expansion meant leveraging Thorny Rose's reputation, design, skills, and supplier relationships to pursue higher-revenue opportunities. Instead of prioritizing constant availability for small retail purchases, they argued the shop should focus more heavily on weddings, wholesale accounts, and large-scale projects that could generate stronger margins without requiring endless hours on the floor.

At Thorny Rose, growth was therefore not simply a question of capacity. It became a negotiation over which performance defined good work and whose definition of success would guide the firm. Julian's availability-centered approach pulled the shop toward constant responsiveness and shared task responsibility. Nicholas's scale-driven approach pushed toward selective projects, higher margins, and operational focus. With no clear authority to reconcile these visions, both stakes remained active. Tension was not episodic, it became routine.

Unlike the other firms, expansion here lacked a single organizing direction. Competing interpretations of the shop's identity produced parallel performances that coexisted in ongoing friction. What follows are two distinct approaches to scaling, each rooted in a different reading of the company's past and its potential future.

Always Be Available: Julian's Vision for Growth

Today's Single Rose Is Tomorrow's Funeral Piece

Julian took pride in offering personal, emotionally attentive service to every customer, regardless of purchase size. Located near several large cemeteries and recommended by funeral homes, Thorny Rose regularly served people buying small bouquets or even a single $3.50 rose for graveside visits. These transactions generated little revenue and required time to add fillers, wrap flowers, and include a complimentary card. For Julian, however, the emotional context justified the investment. When customers mentioned a loss, he would offer condolences and often share stories about his father or other local families. He believed people remembered where they felt heard.

After one customer spent more than ten minutes chatting while buying an $18 arrangement, Julian remarked, "Perhaps this guy is visiting his mom in the hospital today, but in a few months his daughter might need flowers for her wedding." Nicholas immediately challenged him. "Did he tell you his daughter is getting married?" Julian admitted, "No. He didn't even say he had a daughter." Nicholas replied, "Great use of your time." Julian shrugged. "Nicholas, you just never know. You just don't know."

Julian's philosophy was rooted in long-term relational investment. "You never know why a customer has come here until you talk with them," he insisted. "We want them to remember us. As my father would say, you could turn that $5 rose into a $500 funeral piece." Yet these extended conversations often sparked tension. Nicholas frequently accused Julian of "wasting his time," and when Tyler lingered with customers, she was also "scolded." She pushed back, saying, "This is how Julian works with customers, isn't that what we do here?"

The result was confusion about what counted as good service. For Julian, growth meant deepening loyalty through presence and conversation. For others, it raised questions about productivity and scale.

"Stupid Little Arrangements" That Pay Off

Julian emphasized the importance of having ready-made items available for quick purchases, especially small arrangements and Styrofoam crosses with silk flowers for gravesites. He viewed these ready-mades as easy revenue during holidays such as Mother's Day, Easter, and even

Administrative Assistant Day. Before Easter, for example, he repeatedly asked his siblings to prepare gravesite pieces. When they did not, he began making them himself, even though it pulled him away from larger funeral orders.

Nicholas and Lilia chastised him for focusing on "stupid little arrangements" instead of "the big stuff." Julian countered that nothing was ready for Easter. Eventually, he assigned me to make the pieces. The work was more complex than it appeared, from spray-painting the Styrofoam evenly to inserting flowers without damaging the Styrofoam structure.

After the holiday, Julian totaled the sales. The fifteen pieces I sold at $19.95 each generated nearly $300. "Without that," he said, "it's like we're just losing money." For him, preparation and availability were straightforward growth levers. Small sales accumulated. Missed sales compounded.

For his siblings, however, this focus diverted attention from higher-margin projects. Julian's usual tactic of "asking for more and settling for less" failed to build cooperation, so he resorted to direct assignment. The episode revealed both his conviction that growth required constant readiness and his difficulty aligning others around that strategy.

Death Waits for No One

Thorny Rose operates every day of the year, despite repeated requests from other family members to close one day a week, on major holidays like Christmas, or during labor-intensive events such as large weddings. Julian insisted on remaining open. "You know what they say, 'Death waits for no one.' And if the one time someone needs us because a family member passed, and that day we're closed, then that's the experience they have with us." For him, growth required constant availability, even when it strained staff and family life.

When challenged, Julian leaned on his father's familiar refrain. "As my father would say, you never know what tomorrow will bring." As previously noted, these sayings were not rhetorical flourishes; they anchored his strategy in family legacy. Having spent more time working alongside their father and grandfather than other his other siblings, Julian treated uninterrupted service as nonnegotiable.

Nicholas and Lilia initially resisted, citing burnout and the need for boundaries. Over time, however, their objections softened. They conceded it was "probably the best for business." Nicholas acknowledged that customers were often "thankful that we're open because they needed to pick up flowers for an event that day." In practice, Julian's portrayal of availability as both service and virtue carried the day, constraining the flexibility his siblings hoped to introduce into the business.

Nicholas and Lilia's Perspective: Scale, Speed, and High-Value Work

Big Volume, Small Margins—Making Scale Pay

Nicholas frequently argued that their father and grandfather valued diversification. For him this involved expanding Thorny Rose's wholesale business. He preferred "working on bigger projects, on the wholesale stuff" and "developing new relationships with vendors." As he put it, "If we have the capacity to do these sorts of projects, why would I toil all day waiting for someone to wander in the front door. We can do more than that." His strategy emphasized larger orders that reduced dependence on walk-in traffic and allowed him to step away from constant retail service.

Earlier efforts illustrated both the promise and strain of this approach. Thorny Rose invested in equipment to produce dozens of palm crosses for the nearby cemetary for Palm Sunday, selling them wholesale for $8 each. In the first year, they barely broke even due to what Nicholas called "learning curve costs." "We saw how other people made them and copied that," he explained, "but it took us some time." Even after refining the process, margins remained thin and the work was labor-intensive, confirming Julian's warning that wholesale was "not worth the aggravation."

The same logic drove what Nicholas called the "geranium operation," filling large cemetery orders of potted plants. He ran the numbers aloud: $2.50 per plant, 50 cents for baskets, a few cents for bows, sold for $8.50. "We don't make very much individually," he admitted, "but if we make them fast enough, then we can do okay." Speed was everything. Nicholas frequently shouted for workers to "move faster!" and stop being "so sloppy!"

Inside the shop, Julian and Tyler reacted with humor to the intensity. "Oh my god, do you hear Nicholas yelling," Tyler laughed. Julian added, "we think sometimes it's crazy how Nicholas yells at the workers, but when we make just a few bucks on each of these, you can understand why."

For Nicholas, wholesale projects were long-term growth bets built on scale and efficiency. For Julian, they diverted attention from daily customers and delivered modest returns for heavy labor. Although Julian supported the initiatives in principle, he often wished the family would "worry more about some of the other things that need to get done in this place, and not just their own side projects." Nicholas never sought broad cooperation, preferring to manage wholesale operations independently.

Weddings as Growth—When Specialization Disrupts the Shop

Lilia increasingly concentrated on the wedding business, partly to spend more time with her children and partly to avoid daily conflict in the shop.

Julian and Nicholas described it as something she "took on," much like Nicholas assumed responsibility for wholesale work because he "enjoyed it." In the absence of clear coordination, each sibling pursued a different growth lane.

Wedding inquiries were routed to Lilia, whose schedule was irregular. Smaller events under $750 were manageable alone, but larger weddings required help from Junior or other siblings, often during already busy weekends. Nicholas complained that weddings pulled staff away from "more important" work, even though such high-revenue orders would seem to align with his growth ambitions. He argued that "if she just stayed a little later, she could do this on her own." These informal reallocations of labor regularly created friction.

Tension also surfaced around purchasing. Lilia sometimes ordered flowers and accessories for weddings without checking broader shop needs, frustrating Julian. "Why wouldn't you check what else we needed?!" he snapped. Lilia apologized but explained she had rushed to secure limited inventory. Julian insisted she should "place the order for the entire shop. Not just her wedding."

Much of Lilia's time was spent writing quotes, emailing clients, and coordinating logistics. When she asked others to cover phones or assist walk-ins, she was criticized for focusing on "her wedding work" instead of "the work required in the store." She defended herself by noting she handled most of it alone or stayed late to finish. Still, resentment accumulated.

Rather than being framed as a shared strategic shift, weddings became associated with individual preference. By stepping away from the norm of "doing whatever needs to get done," Lilia disrupted shared expectations about responsibility. What began as a path to higher-margin growth became another source of internal strain.

Taken together, Nicholas and Lilia's efforts signaled a broader redefinition of work. Growth shifted from constant availability to selectivity, specialization, and scale. Without clear agreement on that shift, however, specialization felt less like strategy and more like fragmentation.

Performing Growth at Thorny Rose

At Thorny Rose, expansion was not a unified strategic initiative but a struggle over meaning. Julian framed it as deepening the shop's identity around constant availability and emotionally attentive service. Nicholas defined it as scaling into larger, more profitable wholesale work. Lilia pursued weddings as a path toward autonomy and higher-margin specialization. Each approach carried long-term promise. In the absence of a clear authority, no single growth vision became the organizing priority.

Instead, these competing stakes did more than redirect resources. They reshaped what counted as good work. For Julian, answering every phone call and preparing "stupid little arrangements" was an investment in relational loyalty. For Nicholas, speed, volume, and efficiency signaled discipline and seriousness. For Lilia, weddings represented creative control and reputational prestige. Because these definitions were never reconciled, coordination grew strained. Staff time was pulled in multiple directions, and siblings increasingly interpreted one another's initiatives as self-interested rather than shared.

Unlike Rolling Hills, where expansion unsettled volunteer identity, or ElderCare, where it compressed collaborative decision-making, Thorny Rose reveals a different dynamic. When competing growth stakes coexist without clear authority friction becomes structural. The business continued operating but trust thinned and resentment accumulated. Several months after I stopped working regularly at Thorny Rose, Nicholas told me he had stepped back from the firm, taking an "extended vacation" because he felt "underappreciated."

Orienting stakes are not simply revenue goals. They are claims about legacy, identity, and authority. When multiple visions of the future remain unresolved, teams do not merely debate tactics. They renegotiate what the organization is becoming and who has the right to define it.

AeroGears

Ostensive goal: A precise part
Growth orienting stake: Transform from a job shop to a world-class manufacturer
Routine growth performance: Output-driven production and continuous shipping

"We're Still an Infant": Growing Without Building the System

At AeroGears, routine growth centered on becoming a world-class manufacturer by scaling output and securing larger contracts. Unlike the other firms, expansion did not unsettle hierarchy or create competing visions. Authority remained consolidated under Leo and Jack. What changed instead was the rhythm of work. As the push to move from a neighborhood job shop to a "world-class" aerospace manufacturer intensified, production accelerated without a corresponding transformation in coordinating systems. The orienting stake was expansion, but the dominant response was acceleration rather than institutionalization. Volume increased. Pressure mounted. The systems required to sustain that scale lagged behind.

This dynamic surfaced in everyday interactions. After stepping in yet again to override Jack's assignments on the factory floor, Leo turned to me with a smile and asked, "So what do you think about our disorganization?" When I suggested that rapid growth made process stabilization difficult, he replied, "We've been growing for four decade and we're still an infant."

Compared to major aerospace manufacturers, AeroGears remained small in headcount, revenue, and capacity. Yet Leo's ambition was clear. He wanted to transform the firm from a "small parts shop" into "an aerospace company." Alex shared that ambition but defined the path differently. For him, a "world-class operation" meant standardized processes that people consistently followed. Quality required producing precise parts on time, with systems resilient enough that if someone left, "things would correct themselves rather quickly." Building that kind of infrastructure was difficult, especially with "number one" retaining so much centralized control. Still, Alex insisted it was essential. "We shouldn't be a job shop anymore," he said, "but a world-class organization."

Leo, by contrast, equated "world class" with scale. His strategy centered on winning large contracts through aggressive pricing and producing high volumes, even when doing so strained capacity or stretched contract parameters. Growth meant more throughput and bigger customers.

Alex envisioned a different path. AeroGears, he argued, had already mastered basic parts and needed to "get into the next class of jobs." Simple components sold cheaply, but similar parts produced with tighter tolerances and more advanced materials could command $300 per unit. "Those cheap bolts are being purchased from India and China," he warned. "So if you're sitting in an American job shop making nuts for toys, you're not going to be around for much longer." For Alex, scaling required moving upmarket through process discipline, technical capability, and operational consistency.

Unlike Thorny Rose, where competing visions produced visible friction, authority at AeroGears remained consolidated. Alex's expertise fueled frustration about workflow gaps and system weaknesses, but it did not translate into strategic influence. His vision for institutionalizing growth through stronger processes ultimately did not guide the firm's direction.

In his view, the company had already outgrown the job-shop model. "We've had a neighborhood change," he said, and now needed to position itself for higher-end work to avoid becoming an afterthought for "the Boeings of the world." That transition required investment in systems, data-driven planning, and workforce skill. Yet Leo and Jack's centralized control continued to limit how far the organization could shift from acceleration to institutionalization.

"We'll Make What We Can"—When Growth Outpaces Capacity

Pushing Volume, Losing Control

To break into the aerospace supply chain, Leo routinely submitted aggressively low bids so intermediary firms could "test AeroGears out," as Jack explained. Rather than pricing conservatively or building in sufficient production time, he accepted more work than the shop could reliably handle.

In one recent case, AeroGears shipped "bad parts." Alex described the episode as "just embarrassing." The company absorbed a financial loss and risked losing future contracts "because we blew it." For Alex, whose professional identity centered on quality assurance, the failure was not just operational. It was personal.

He traced the breakdown to Leo's constant pressure on the factory floor. "Leo kept going down and asking, 'How far along are we? When are we going to get done?'" Workers rushed, "didn't follow protocol exactly, and there you go." Under routine conditions, the shop's "stick-to-your-task" performance functioned well when Jack maintained control over workflow. But when Leo inserted urgency into the process, coordination frayed and errors multiplied.

As Alex put it, Leo was "a glutton, so he's going to take everything that comes his way." Growth prioritized volume without disciplined capacity planning. The result was compromised quality, financial setbacks, and erosion of the very procedures meant to protect standards.

"If We're Late, We're Late"—Normalizing Incomplete Orders

As aerospace contracts increased, late deliveries became routine. Staffing constraints mattered, but tracking was the larger issue. Jack's "magical yellow pad" could no longer manage the growing flow of parts.

Under one contract, AeroGears was expected to produce sixteen complex components per month for NTW Group. AeroGears frequently failed to complete full orders on time. Alex reiterated his position, arguing that it was "better to deliver a perfect product late than an imperfect product on time." Jack took a different view. When deadlines slipped, he would say, "We're going to make as many as we can today and then PO it." To "PO it" meant shipping what was finished using UPS Red, next-day air service that cost far more than standard ground shipping.

One morning, I overheard Colleen on the phone with her counterpart, Jerome, at NTW. She explained they had eleven pieces ready and would send the rest the following week. Jerome told her to ship what they had and close the order. Next month's quantity could be increased to make up the difference. After hanging up, Colleen remarked, "The motto at AeroGears is now, 'if we're late, we're late. What we have done, we have done. And that's it.' This is what Jack wants...so this is what we do."

The commitment to producing precise parts remained intact. Quality was still nonnegotiable. What shifted was completeness. Under growth pressure, shipping partial orders became normalized. The ostensive goal did not change, but its enactment did. Good work was redefined in practice. Precision was protected, and delivery reliability became elastic. Even Colleen, who often seemed detached, recognized that the company was falling short of its own expectations.

When the Buffer Disappears: Late Parts, No Slack, and Rising Risk

Missed deadlines had become a growing liability at AeroGears. "We have the same bottlenecks with the production flow like other companies have," Keith observed, "but we don't figure out how to solve it." On-time delivery had dropped to roughly 90 percent, well below the industry standard of 96–98 percent. "Now we're on probation with NTW," he added. Late shipments also jeopardized AeroGears' AS9100 accreditation. Despite repeated conversations, Keith felt stuck, saying, "We're not learning how to correct the issue even though we talk about it all the time."

Even as delays mounted, AeroGears continued bidding on new NTW work. Keith acknowledged the contradiction. "They're not really considering us for new things...and why should they if we can't get our current parts to them on time?" Previously, a buyer at NTW named Shawn managed delays by adjusting due dates. After Shawn retired, Jerome took over and "he's unwilling to push any due date back." Keith reflected, "Did we honestly think that that was going to go on like that forever?"

The informal buffer had disappeared. Leo's relationships with senior NTW executives continued to shield the company from immediate consequences, but those ties could not offset sustained performance gaps. Increased scrutiny would likely expose the underlying weaknesses.

Keith understood the risk acutely. Having previously worked at NTW, he recalled a common refrain, "There's only two Boeings but there's hundreds of little guys they could use." Underperforming suppliers were replaceable. Now he found himself part of the "dispensable small manufacturer" he once joked about. Although he raised concerns in meetings with Leo and Jack, he described those discussions as "useless." Repeated delays clashed with his professional pride and deepened his disillusionment with how growth was being pursued.

"The Word Document to Nowhere": Performing Organizational Order Without Coordination

To improve production tracking, Jack asked Fred, Keith, and me to build an Excel file linked to daily Word documents showing where each part sat in the process. The tool was meant to provide real-time updates for staff and for NTW during "Milestone Report" visits, replacing Jack's "magical yellow pad" for this client, at least in theory. Keith predicted it would "add confusion to the system, not clarity," and Alex admitted he "would never look to that system for an accurate account of works in progress anyway."

After days spent constructing the spreadsheet, Keith finally asked, "Look how many personnel hours have already devoted to this...we still don't really know what the purpose is." I knew the underlying scheduling and flow problems required the software upgrade Leo had originally hired me to design. The Word-to-Excel setup felt like theater, signaling organization rather than creating it.

When pressed, Jack explained the reports would allow others to answer customer questions without checking with him. The intention was reasonable. The execution was not. Maintaining multiple documents took longer than simply asking Jack. When Keith asked whether the data would be used for planning and due dates, Jack replied, "There's no point in putting in a projected due date because it's meaningless." Work, he insisted, got done "when someone has the time." Planning was "a futile exercise."

This was the turning point. The system was not about operational control; it was about appearances. We had assumed the data would inform bidding decisions and realistic timelines. Instead, it had no strategic function. As Keith put it, "If Jack doesn't believe that we can actually create any order through capturing data, then of course we'll never fix any of the problems here."

Despite our skepticism, we complied. Over time, we left sections of the Word documents incomplete to see whether the system was being used. No one noticed. The Excel file was updated for NTW meetings, but the detailed reports went untouched.

AeroGears continued missing deadlines while pursuing new contracts. The "Word Document to Nowhere," as we began calling it, symbolized a broader pattern in which growth was pursued through acceleration and symbolic organization rather than structural redesign. The shop appeared busier and more systematized, but the underlying coordination problems remained intact.

Performing Growth at AeroGears

Alex repeatedly argued, "This company has a lot of potential, but they're not in a place to keep up. Look, we're falling behind on orders. That's not good for us." For him, scaling meant investing in formal processes that would allow AeroGears to operate as a truly "world-class" manufacturer. In his view, the prevailing approach of producing as many parts as possible and "PO it" was inadequate. Declining on-time performance embarrassed him professionally and signaled deeper structural weakness. If key individuals left, he warned, "it'll fall apart...because so much of the information...has not yet been institutionalized."

Yet Alex understood the limits of his influence. "At the end of the day, when quality reviews come, you know my stuff is in order," he said, retreating to a stick-to-your-task routine even as he pushed for broader change. Jack's assertive control over operations, backed by Leo, made coalition-building risky. Those who challenged the status quo were unlikely to prevail.

AeroGears continued winning contracts, but expansion did not produce institutional maturity. Instead, it amplified the firm's dependence on centralized authority and informal coordination. The tracking documents we privately called "smoke and mirrors" reinforced the perception that leadership was signaling organization rather than building it. Output rose. Systems lagged. Employees complied, but without conviction.

The result was not failure but fragility. AeroGears grew in scale without growing in coordination, accelerating production without embedding the processes required to sustain a world-class operation. Growth preserved momentum, but it did not resolve the structural gaps that momentum exposed.

Chapter 16

The Logic of Growth

Leading When Identity Is in Motion

Generating order during routine growth proved difficult across all four firms. Expansion did not unfold through deliberate strategy or coordinated planning. It emerged opportunistically, when new contracts, clients, or revenue streams appeared. Because growth was typically reactive rather than collectively negotiated, leaders rarely anticipated how it would reshape shared meanings, work identities, or cohesion. Norms loosened, yet new alignments did not fully form.

Across the cases, a persistent tension surfaced—the need to expand without losing what made each organization who it was. At Rolling Hills, diversification risked turning a relational farm into a transactional enterprise. At ElderCare, taking on more clients intensified risk and compressed care routines. At Thorny Rose, larger projects magnified coordination pressures and authority fractures. At AeroGears, scaling output strained precision and exposed weak institutional systems. These were not smooth transitions. They were imperfect growth performances shaped by each firm's orienting stakes.

Because growth decisions were concentrated among those with formal authority, lower-status employees were often excluded from conversations that shaped change. Expansion arrived as new demands rather than shared direction. Without deliberate interpretation, coordination frayed and frustration accumulated.

This mattered because work identities are socially constructed. Identity is grounded in group loyalty and interaction. When growth altered valued routines and definitions of competence, employees experienced misalignment. At AeroGears, a resistance coalesced into an informal coalition. At ElderCare, staff pushed back against placement decisions. At Rolling Hills, Aiko left. At Thorny Rose, Nicholas withdrew. In each case, identity strain preceded disengagement.

Growth also normalized compromise. At Rolling Hills, communal ideals strained under monetization. At ElderCare, careful aide-client matching

DOI: 10.4324/9781003779803-20

gave way to speed. At Thorny Rose, shared labor norms fractured under specialization. At AeroGears, adherence to delivery commitments eroded under production pressure. Expansion was meant to strengthen these firms. Instead, it often destabilized the cultural foundations that had previously made coordination possible.

Why Meaning Management Determines Whether Growth Holds

Growth is not merely operational change. It is cultural reorganization. It reshapes what feels important, alters work identities, and redistributes authority. Whether that reorganization strengthens or fractures a team depends on leadership's capacity to manage meaning. Periods of expansion require social skill. Leaders must frame change in ways that resonate with existing identities, justify trade-offs, and help employees reinterpret evolving roles. Authority can mandate new procedures, but it cannot create shared purpose on its own.

Across these firms, leaders often relied on positional authority to push growth forward. That authority enabled action, but it did not generate alignment. When leaders failed to connect expansion to team identity, resistance followed. Lower-status employees sometimes acted as informal institutional entrepreneurs, mobilizing established cultural expectations to push back against growth initiatives. These struggles revealed both the durability of local idiocultures and the difficulty of reshaping them without shared ownership of change.

As Alice observed, "things can't stay the same." Yet organizational adaptation is never purely operational. It is relational and symbolic. Sustainable growth requires more than opportunity and ambition. It requires deliberate attention to meaning, identity, and the cultural rhythms that allow teams to adapt without losing coherence.

Small firms often falter not because of poor strategy, but because they neglect meaning during expansion. When leaders treat growth primarily as a problem of capacity, staffing, systems, and logistics, expansion becomes disruption. When they engage identity, invite interpretation, and build shared understanding, growth becomes transformation.

Routine growth performance captures this distinction. It is how teams pursue expansion without abandoning who they are. It holds when leaders and informal institutional entrepreneurs align new ambitions with shared values through shared interpretation. It fragments when growth is imposed through authority alone and identity is stretched beyond what the group can recognize as its own.

Nine Questions to Reveal Your Team's Growth Culture

During growth, organizations do not simply expand operations. They unsettle the social order that once made coordination feel natural. As orienting stakes shift toward new opportunities, routines stretch, roles blur, and long-standing meanings of good work are renegotiated. Unlike crises, growth does not automatically unite teams around a shared threat. It introduces ambiguity about priorities, identity, and fairness that must be actively managed. How leaders frame change and invite participation often determines whether growth strengthens culture or fractures it.

The questions below help surface how teams are actually performing growth in everyday interaction.

See the Pattern: What Changes as Growth Pressure Rises

1 **When orienting stakes shift toward growth, what routines break first?** Is it communication, training, handoffs, standards, or coordination? Why that one? What does its strain reveal about how the team was originally structured?

2 **Which kinds of work become invisible during expansion?** Who absorbs onboarding, cleanup, coordination, emotional labor, or customer recovery? Which contributions are essential yet unrecognized? How does that invisibility shape morale and perceptions of fairness?

3 **Who is stretched the most as volume increases?** How do they interpret what that stretch signals about their role and value? What boundary conflicts emerge over authority, time, or responsibility? How are those disputes resolved, and by whom?

Understand the Stakes: What Growth Reveals About Identity

4 **What trade-offs does the team believe growth requires?** What is being traded for scale? Where are time, quality, autonomy, relationships, or pride in work beginning to erode? What now counts as success? Which values are slipping to the margins?

5 **What story does the team tell itself when growth accelerates?** Do people default to scripts such as "just ship it," "figure it out later," "take every opportunity," or "protect the craft"? Who promotes that narrative? Who resists it? How does that story shape coordination?

6 **Where is identity strain most visible?** Where do people say, "This isn't who we are" or "This isn't good work"? What moments trigger defensiveness or nostalgia? Which routines feel most threatened by expansion?

Shift the Performance: Make Expansion Sustainable

7 **Where does growth create the appearance of control without improving coordination?**
Which dashboards, meetings, or reports signal order without changing workflow? What feels like progress but operates as organizational theater rather than capacity building?

8 **Who manages meaning during growth transitions?**
Who frames trade-offs and explains shifting priorities? Who introduces new routines or redefines roles in ways that feel legitimate? Where do informal institutional entrepreneurs begin to surface?

9 **What will be gained, and what might be lost, if expansion remains the dominant stake?**
Which cultural strengths or identities feel most at risk over the next six months? What relationships, norms, or standards could erode? How can leaders protect what matters while still scaling?

Finale

Chapter 17

Becoming a Master Performer

Setting the Tempo of Team Culture

Culture grows where people have time, autonomy, and repeated opportunities to work together. It cannot be installed by leaders or captured in a statement. It is interpreted and negotiated through shared experience, the ordinary moments in which people coordinate, adjust, and respond to one another. Leaders who want strong cultures must protect space for relationships to form and recognize that meaning emerges through practice, not proclamation.

In daily work, employees rarely consult job descriptions or strategy decks to decide how to act. They rely on shared performance routines developed over time inside teams. Formal tools matter only insofar as they are filtered through lived experience and collective sensemaking.

Culture, then, is what teams come to understand together about how to produce good work under shifting conditions.

Ostensive goals anchor what good work looks like. At Rolling Hills, that meant tasty and attractive produce. At ElderCare, it meant compassionate care. At Thorny Rose, it meant beautiful arrangements. At AeroGears, it meant producing precise parts. These shared understandings provided each team with a simple, enduring picture of success.

What changed was not the ostensive goal itself but how it was enacted under shifting orienting stakes. Throughout this book, I argued that ostensive goals take shape through three recurring cultural performances, or rhythms, namely routine stability, routine crisis, and routine growth. Each is activated by a different stake, carries a distinct tempo, generates its own emotional charge, and reshapes the team's behavior scripts for how work should be done.

Routine stability is marked by predictability. It preserves coherence in the present, allowing teams to rely on settled patterns, familiar identities, and shared confidence in what good work looks like. Work feels natural, familiar, and largely unquestioned because coordination has become habitual. Routine crisis compresses coordination around immediate threat, narrowing attention and tightening authority to prevent loss. Its pace is urgent. Its emotional

DOI: 10.4324/9781003779803-22

register is heightened. The goal remains the same, but its defense becomes paramount. Routine growth stretches coordination toward an imagined future, asking teams to reinterpret who they are and what their work is becoming. Its orientation is expansive and anticipatory. Its emotional charge is hopeful but destabilizing. The goal remains, yet its meaning is renegotiated.

Stability preserves coherence. Crisis defends it. Growth redefines it.

Crises and growth destabilize the routine stability equilibrium by activating orienting stakes. Demands for speed, scale, or protection force renegotiation of roles, authority, and expectations. These shifts are shaped by group histories and idiocultures, the local systems of meaning that guide interpretation and response.

Culture is not static. It is dynamic and negotiated, shaped through shared norms, emotional expectations, and everyday interaction. Leadership within that process is less about control than about participation. Master performers do not create the rhythm. They attune to it, adjust it, and help others move together through stability, crisis, and growth without losing the shared meaning that makes coordination possible.

Setting the Tempo of Work

Leadership is not simply about designing the right system, declaring a direction, and stepping back. The most effective leaders do something subtler and far more powerful. They set tempo.

Rhythm gives work its underlying pattern. Tempo determines how fast, slow, or intensely that pattern is performed in response to shifting stakes. The rhythms teams develop allow people to realign as conditions change, guiding coordination as everyday work takes new forms.

Watch a great DJ work a room. They do not follow a rigid playlist or blast the same energy all night. They read the crowd. When the floor is calm, they ease people into a familiar beat. When momentum builds, they raise the intensity. When chaos threatens, they steady the tempo. The art is not selecting the perfect song. It is sensing what the moment requires and shaping the flow, so people move together. Leadership works the same way.

Inside every organization, work unfolds in rhythms. There are periods of routine stability when teams rely on settled patterns. There are moments of crisis when pressure spikes and coordination must tighten. There are stretches of growth when old routines no longer fit and new ones must emerge. High-performing leaders do not manage each moment with the same tone or tools. They shift tempo. They know when to slow for clarity, when to accelerate for action, and when to hold steady so teams do not spin out of control.

This is what it means to become a master performer.

Across the four organizations in this book, success did not hinge on perfectly designed strategies or carefully crafted culture statements. It depended on the way leaders and teams adjusted the pace and intensity of work as conditions changed, and how those adjustments reshaped interaction, negotiation, resistance, and shared meaning. When leaders misread the situation, tension rose, burnout followed, and performance suffered. When they aligned rhythm with reality and created space for teams to interpret change together, teams moved with surprising coordination and resilience.

Importantly, this did not happen through command and control. It happened through soft power rooted in legitimacy, trust, and shared meaning built through everyday interaction. Like a DJ whose influence comes not from shouting instructions but from guiding the beat, effective leaders shaped behavior by reinforcing norms, clarifying orienting stakes, and helping teams interpret shifting demands. Their authority felt natural because it was grounded in the culture the team had built together.

Anyone who has been part of an organization attempting to change its culture knows how difficult it becomes when leaders view themselves as architects of culture. The durability of social orders explains why culture resists top-down redesign. Leaders cannot create culture ex nihilo. Announcing new values such as openness or psychological safety accomplishes little if everyday interaction remains unchanged. If interruptions continue, dissent is discouraged, or mistakes are remembered selectively, employees quickly learn that the values are symbolic rather than real. Culture cannot be rolled out or transformed through a single initiative. It shifts through repeated adjustments in everyday interaction over time.

Becoming a master performer, then, is not about working harder, issuing clearer directives, or installing better systems. It is about learning to read the room. It requires understanding the cultural rhythms already operating inside teams and knowing how to guide them through calm, pressure, and change. Leaders who do this well sustain coordination, motivation, and resilience without relying on constant oversight.

The interaction order described in this book is not unique to the cases examined here. While the underlying rhythms of work appear across organizations, their expression varies by context. The sections ahead explore what this means in practice for entrepreneurs, growing firms, large enterprises, remote teams, and investors.

Advice for Entrepreneurs: Build Culture Before You Build Structure

For entrepreneurs, culture begins forming the moment people start working together. Long before formal roles, processes, or strategies take shape, early routines establish foundational norms about responsibility, communication, conflict, and commitment. Founders often rush to install structure, assuming clarity comes from rules and systems. But ethnographic evidence suggests meaning comes first. Teams learn how work happens through shared experience, not policy documents.

Early friction should not be feared or suppressed. It is a resource. It surfaces expectations, clarifies boundaries, and shapes collective identity. When founders make implicit assumptions explicit and turn everyday coordination into shared language, they build the cultural foundation that will carry the business forward.

At this stage, leadership depends less on formal authority or control and more on soft power, influence rooted in legitimacy, trust, and shared meaning. Soft power lives in the unwritten rules of the interaction order. Entrepreneurs cultivate it by consistently aligning their actions with shared values, demonstrating fairness and competence, and showing genuine investment in the team's success. Because it emerges through repeated interaction, it feels natural rather than imposed. It cannot be declared; it must be earned.

In young ventures especially, early team development sets the scripts for how people collaborate, respond to stress, and define what good work looks like. Structure will come. But culture, once formed, is far harder to rewrite.

Advice for Growing the Small Business: Learn to Shift Cultural Performances

As small businesses grow, the challenge is not merely scaling operations. It is learning when and how to shift cultural performances. What sustains routine stability often falters under crisis or expansion. Growth destabilizes shared meaning. New hires arrive. Workloads intensify. Long-standing routines strain under new demands.

Leaders who treat growth as acceleration alone often create confusion, burnout, and conflict. Effective founders should become cultural stewards. They help teams adapt routines without losing coherence. They invite collaborative adapation, encouraging employees to interpret new challenges and participate in shaping emerging practices. Shared interpretation builds commitment. Commitment sustains resilience.

Formal structure has a role in this phase, but only when used deliberately. Policies and procedures can clarify expectations and reduce bias. They cannot substitute for lived culture. When formalization lacks social legitimacy, it produces symbolic compliance rather than real coordination. Structure strengthens performance when it fits how people work, not when it disrupts established rhythms.

As organizations expand, authority naturally increases. Influence, however, still depends on credibility and alignment with team norms. Growth holds when leaders cultivate trust and shared meaning alongside new systems. It falters when positional control replaces cultural stewardship.

Advice for Executives of Large Organizations: Lead Through Teams, Not Systems

Even in the largest organizations, real work happens in small teams. Departments, project groups, and operational units develop distinct micro-cultures shaped by shared history, emotional tone, humor, and informal power. These idiocultures strongly influence how people respond to routine work, crisis, change initiatives, and leadership decisions. Treating an organization as a single, unified culture obscures this variation. Effective executives recognize these differences and lead through them, allowing local interpretation of goals while aligning incentives and values at the enterprise level.

Onboarding and identity formation are especially critical in large firms. New employees do not absorb culture from manuals or orientation slides. They learn it through participation. When onboarding relies primarily on formal programs, newcomers are left to decode norms on their own and often replicate existing dysfunctions. Belonging and commitment emerge through repeated interaction, mentorship, and shared practice. Effective onboarding unfolds over time and creates structured opportunities to observe, contribute, and reflect within and across teams.

Executives should resist the impulse to manage complexity with ever more elaborate systems. Complexity rarely disappears. It simply migrates. Instead, leaders should articulate simple, robust ostensive goals that remain stable even as conditions shift. Their power lies in clarity. Ostensive goals anchor coordination while allowing flexibility in how work is performed under changing stakes. When goals become overly complex or frequently revised, alignment erodes and meaning frays. Simplicity provides coherence. Cultural rhythms provide adaptability. Strategy becomes real not through detailed plans alone but through everyday interaction.

Executives must recognize that every strategy, policy, or structural change will be interpreted through local team cultures. Employees do not implement initiatives as written. They filter them through past experience, current relationships, and shared understandings of what truly matters. This is why identical corporate programs can produce dramatically different outcomes across departments. Effective leaders anticipate this interpretive process and engage managers in building a shared understanding rather than assuming compliance will follow communication.

One of the most underdeveloped capabilities in large organizations is social skill—the ability to read group dynamics, frame situations in ways that resonate with identity and history, and realign coordination as stakes shift. Leadership development often emphasizes technical expertise, financial acumen, and performance management. Far less attention is devoted to meaning management. Yet team leaders must know how to surface tensions, interpret resistance, and rebuild shared purpose when routines are unsettled. These skills can be strengthened through coaching, reflective work on live team challenges, peer learning cohorts, and scenario-based training focused on coordination under pressure.

Leaders with strong social skill should be empowered as institutional entrepreneurs. They understand when to assert direction, when to widen participation, and when to allow adaptation to emerge organically. Resistance, when it appears, is rarely a rejection of authority. More often, it reflects an effort to protect the meaning of work and the identities built through routine practice. Executives who recognize this dynamic can channel adaptation rather than provoke opposition.

Taken together, these patterns show why leadership in large organizations is less about designing perfect systems and more about guiding coordination as cultural performances evolve. Policies signal intent, but teams translate them into practice. Strategies set direction, but rhythms of interaction determine execution. As orienting stakes shift, leaders who can set tempo, manage meaning, and work within existing cultural repertoires are far more likely to sustain performance than those who rely on positional control alone.

Advice for Managing Remote and Hybrid Teams: Make Culture Visible When Interaction Is Distributed

Remote and hybrid work do not eliminate culture. They change where cultural performances unfold. The same processes of coordination, shared interpretation, and negotiated routines still drive performance, but the interaction order becomes harder to read and easier to fragment. Without shared physical space, urgency is misinterpreted, engagement drifts, and coordination can unravel.

Leaders who treat remote work as a technology problem miss the deeper challenge. It is cultural. In distributed settings, leaders must intentionally protect space for repeated interaction because culture grows through ongoing contact, not occasional check-ins. Short, regular rhythms of collaboration and reflection often matter more than long but infrequent formal meetings. When communication becomes purely transactional, shared meaning thins and performance suffers.

Soft power becomes even more central when physical oversight disappears. Influence flows through legitimacy, trust, and consistency rather than proximity or authority. Employees pay close attention to who is heard in virtual meetings, how leaders respond under pressure, and whether commitments are honored. Tempo management is also amplified. Some teams drift into constant urgency. Others slow into quiet disengagement. Master performers shape rhythm by clarifying priorities, protecting focus time, and aligning orienting stakes so urgency is purposeful rather than perpetual.

Finally, leaders must actively manage meaning. Without informal conversations that help people make sense of change, assumptions multiply. Naming expectations, surfacing tensions, and reinforcing what good work looks like keep teams aligned as routines shift. Remote work succeeds not through tighter monitoring or better tools but through deliberate cultivation of interaction, rhythm, trust, and shared purpose.

Advice for Investors and Venture Capitalists: Culture Is the Operating System of Growth

For investors, culture is not a peripheral accessory to strategy. It is the operating system through which execution runs. Financial capital and market opportunity do not generate performance on their own. Teams do. Ventures succeed or stall based on how well people coordinate, adapt, resolve conflict, and make sense of pressure together.

Cultural inefficiencies rarely appear first on financial statements. They surface in founder burnout, operational chaos, repeated misalignment, and stalled execution. Overwork, injury, leadership withdrawal, or simmering cofounder resentment are not merely personal issues. They are early warning signals of organizational strain. By the time performance metrics decline, the cultural foundation has often already weakened.

Investors who attend to team dynamics gain a powerful diagnostic advantage. Beyond reviewing strategy decks and growth projections, they should observe interaction patterns. How are decisions made? How is disagreement handled? How are newcomers integrated? Does influence flow through trust and legitimacy, or only through authority? How do leaders frame setbacks and shifting stakes?

Strong cultures distribute responsibility, sustain resilience, and enable adaptation as complexity increases. Weak cultures concentrate pressure at the top, breed disengagement, and erode execution. The most scalable ventures are not simply those with strong products or market timing. They are those with teams capable of repeatedly recreating effective coordination as growth stretches identity, routines, and authority.

From Insight to Action: Leading Inside Team Culture

Although these insights vary in application across entrepreneurs, growing firms, large organizations, remote teams, and investors, they converge on a single truth. Performance rises and falls with the rhythms of everyday interaction inside teams. Culture is not a background condition. It is the medium through which work happens. The question, then, is not whether culture matters, but how leaders can work with it in real time. How do you read the rhythm? How do you recognize shifting orienting stakes? How do you intervene without undermining legitimacy?

What follows translates these ideas into practical actions leaders can take immediately to strengthen coordination, resilience, and shared meaning.

Start Where Culture Lives: Watch the Interaction Order

Before launching another initiative, run a simple diagnostic in your next meeting. Your team's culture changes predictably as stakes shift. Stability, crisis, and growth each activate different scripts, authority patterns, and definitions of good work. Identify which performance is unfolding, then observe:

- Who speaks first and who never does
- Who interrupts and who gets interrupted
- Who gets the "benefit of the doubt" after mistakes
- Which concerns get taken seriously and which get labeled "negative"
- Where decisions actually happen (in the room, after the meeting, in side conversations)
- How conflict is handled (debated, avoided, joked away, escalated, punished)

You are not looking for villains. You are looking for patterns. Culture is repetition. When you can name the pattern without shaming individuals, you create the possibility for change.

Assume Plans Fail at the "Translation Layer"

Leaders should assume that plans are most likely to break down where strategy meets everyday action. Initiatives rarely fail because employees do not care or are actively resisting change. More often, they falter because teams are left to improvise the "how" without shared meaning, clear trade-offs, or coordinating routines.

This is why culture cannot be treated as something an organization simply "has." It operates as a set of performances that teams shift into as stakes change. When a new priority is introduced without guidance on how it reshapes daily work, people default to familiar scripts they already trust.

To surface breakdowns at the translation layer, ask two simple questions:

- What does this priority mean for your day-to-day decisions?
- What trade-offs are you being forced to make to deliver it?

If people struggle to answer, the issue is not resistance. It is ambiguity. And when ambiguity dominates, teams retreat to the routines they already trust.

Protect Routine Stability Like It's an Asset (Because It Is)

Routine stability is not the enemy of innovation or growth. It is the foundation that makes coordinated work possible. The shared expectations teams develop over time reduce friction, limit constant renegotiation, and allow people to move quickly and confidently together.

Leaders often undermine this stability unintentionally. In the name of improvement, they tweak roles, shift priorities, and revise processes without accounting for the cultural cost. Each small change introduces confusion, duplicated effort, and mounting friction that slowly undermine collective effectiveness.

Master performers respond differently. They deliberately identify and protect what anchors coordination, including the following:

- One or two core routines that structure daily work
- One or two nonnegotiable standards, like quality, safety, client care, or mutual respect, that should never be part of a trade-off

Naming these boundaries explicitly creates the stability that allows teams to absorb change without losing coherence. Stability is not the absence of adaptation. It is the structure that makes adaptation survivable.

Centralize During Crisis, Then Repair Deliberately

In moments of crisis, teams often require tighter authority and faster decision-making. This is not authoritarianism. It is triage. When stakes are high and time is scarce, temporarily centralizing action can protect what matters most and restore stability.

The cultural risk emerges afterward. Trouble begins when leaders fail to explain why normal routines were suspended or neglect to help the team interpret what changed. Without deliberate sensemaking, temporary measures harden into habit and urgency becomes the default mode of operation.

Skilled leaders pair short-term centralization with intentional repair.

Preparation matters. Before crisis strikes, establish shared expectations for how authority will shift under pressure. Teams should know when decisions will centralize, how stakes will be framed, and when reflection will follow. During recovery, debriefs should focus not only on what went wrong but on what it meant. What losses were considered unacceptable? What did the team worked hardest to protect? Which rules shifted under pressure, and which now return? These conversations restore shared understanding and rebuild trust. They allow teams to return to a sustainable rhythm rather than remaining trapped in perpetual urgency.

Treat Growth as Identity Work, Not Just Operational Work

Growth does not simply stretch operational capacity. It reshapes how people understand their work and who they are within the organization. What is this place becoming? What is growth asking me to become? What counts as good work now?

As roles expand, routines shift, and expectations rise, employees confront deeper questions about identity and what their place in the organization will become. When leaders push expansion without creating a shared understanding of why change is necessary, teams may comply in the short term but disengage over time. Growth begins to feel imposed, incoherent, or dismissive of the group's craft and history, especially when people are asked to do more without renegotiating what support and standards accompany those demands.

The strongest leaders treat growth as identity work as much as operational work. They explicitly engage teams in conversations about the new skills required, the evolving standards of excellence, and the trade-offs expansion entails. They clarify what will change and what will remain protected. When these tensions are named, they can be addressed. When they remain unspoken, resistance surfaces through cynicism, disengagement, and eventual turnover.

Avoid "Growth Theater" by Renegotiating the Informal Contract

One of the most common leadership failures during periods of expansion is growth theater. Leaders introduce new dashboards, systems, rituals, and narratives that signal progress without improving how work gets done. Visibility increases, but capacity does not.

A simple diagnostic separates infrastructure from theater. Ask whether the change improves handoffs, scheduling, training, decision rights, or real capacity. If it does not, it creates the appearance of control without improving coordination. Over time, employees see the gap. Trust erodes.

The deeper issue beneath growth theater is a failure to renegotiate the informal contract. As growth accelerates, workloads expand, expectations rise, and roles blur. Yet the implicit agreements governing effort, fairness, and support often remain unspoken and unchanged. When leaders add responsibilities without acknowledging these shifts, growth feels less like opportunity and more like breach.

Renegotiation only works when it is made explicit. Leaders must name the shifts clearly and concretely. They should say:

- "Here's what's changing."
- "Here's why it matters."
- "Here's what we're taking off your plate."
- "Here's what authority and support you'll gain."
- "Here's what we will not compromise."

Leaders who navigate growth well treat it as both an operational and relational transition. They distinguish between systems that improve coordination and those that merely display activity. Growth grounded in renegotiation builds capacity and commitment. Growth that skips it becomes theater.

Treat Resistance as a Signal of Cultural Protection

Across the organizations in this book, those who resisted change were rarely simply difficult or uncooperative. Informal challengers often emerged when growth initiatives threatened core identities, standards, or sources of pride in work. Statements such as "this isn't what we're here for" or "that's not real quality" reflected efforts to protect dignity, mission, and craft, not personal convenience. Attempts to purchase short-term compliance through incentives or perks rarely resolve this deeper tension. They often produced moral fatigue and eventual exit.

The best leaders treat resistance as information about what the team values most. It signals what people are trying to preserve. Rather than dismissing dissent, engage it by asking:

- "What are you trying to protect?"
- "How do we protect that while still moving?"

By inviting dissenters into design conversations, leaders can channel friction into constructive adaptation. Ignoring resistance does not eliminate it. It drives concerns underground, where they take shape as withdrawal, cynicism, or organized opposition.

Lead Like a Meaning Manager: Frame, Translate, and Align

If "culture architect" suggests designing culture from above, meaning management reflects something more realistic. Leaders shape interpretation. They protect identities. They create space for teams to negotiate new scripts. Your role is to frame what is changing, why it is changing, what will remain protected, and how people will be supported. Then create structured opportunities for teams to interpret and adapt together.

Adopt three framing habits:

- Name the stakes: What are we protecting? What becomes possible?
- Name the trade-offs: What will we sacrifice? What will we not?
- Name the tempo: Are we tightening, loosening, experimenting, or stabilizing?

People do not need perfect certainty. They need coherent sensemaking. When leaders create the conditions for it, coordination strengthens even in the face of uncertainty.

Learn to DJ the Team's Tempo

None of the leaders in this book mastered these practices all the time. In fact, many struggled. But the moments when they were most effective shared a common pattern: they sensed the rhythm of their teams and adjusted the tempo without breaking cohesion.

At their best, they knew when to tighten authority and when to loosen it, when to slow down for repair and collective reflection, and when to push forward through experimentation and growth. They recognized when to centralize decisions, when to widen participation, when to stretch routines, and when to protect the patterns that kept the system coherent.

Leadership is most powerful not when strategy is flawless, but when timing is right. Not when leaders control every move, but when they guide the beat so others can move together.

Leading Through Everyday Rhythms

Culture takes shape in everyday interaction, not in vision statements, core values, or performance metrics. Those tools may signal intent, but they rarely generate the deep coordination, trust, and shared meaning that sustained performance requires. What holds teams together is not messaging. It is the repeated ways people coordinate work, build relationships, respond to pressure, and interpret what is happening around them.

Leaders influence culture by shaping the conditions under which these patterns form and change. They do so by participating in the interaction order of work, negotiating meaning alongside others, and responding to the constraints culture itself imposes. Culture is not built once and managed from above. It is continuously produced through practice.

Across the organizations in this book, employees learned what mattered, what was risky, and what counted as competent action not from manuals or formal training but from watching one another navigate everyday problems. Expectations traveled through stories, humor, conflict, and shared responses to challenge. Culture was not delivered. It was enacted.

Over time, these interactions formed distinct rhythms for routine work, moments of crisis, and periods of growth. These rhythms were durable, often invisible, and deeply consequential. They shaped whether teams adapted smoothly or stalled, collaborated or fragmented, and experienced change as manageable or chaotic. Improving performance does not begin with launching a culture initiative. It begins with noticing how work is actually performed day to day.

Master performers do not impose an entirely new beat. They lead more like skilled DJs, working with the rhythms already in motion. They read the room. They adjust tempo when stakes rise, steady the group after disruption, and protect enough stability so growth does not dissolve into chaos. They reinforce routines that strengthen coordination and deliberately reshape those that undermine it.

In the end, organizational success is not about declaring a "great culture." It is about sustaining coordination as conditions change. It is about preserving trust under pressure, adapting without losing identity, and guiding teams through shifting stakes without breaking the shared meaning that makes collective work possible.

Acknowledgments

Support for a book like *Hidden Rhythms of Teams* comes from the many teams an author belongs to along the way. No one writes alone. Ideas are shaped in conversation, sharpened through disagreement, and sustained by small acts of encouragement that accumulate over time. This book grew not only from fieldwork but also from years of shared effort with people who showed me how coordination, trust, and meaning are built in everyday work.

The questions that animate this book trace back to my family, my first team. My parents, Harriet and Allan, and my brother, Adam, offered steady encouragement throughout graduate school and beyond. They listened carefully, asked difficult questions, and pushed me to clarify my thinking. Conversations with my father about his experiences in business—where workplace realities aligned with management theory and where they diverged—helped me see the gaps that eventually became research questions.

My dissertation co-chairs, Dr. Paul McLean and Dr. Deborah Dougherty, saw promise in this project early and helped give it structure, offering detailed feedback and encouraging me to pursue the integration of sociology and management. I am also grateful to the other members of my committee, including Dr. Deborah Carr, Dr. Hana Shephard, and especially Dr. Torsten Pieper, who introduced himself to a young PhD student at a conference and affirmed that ethnographic research in small businesses was not only viable but valuable.

I owe a deep debt to the owners, managers, and employees of the four firms at the heart of this book. It takes courage to grant a researcher full access to an organization, including its missteps and successes, as well as its humor and its conflict. By welcoming me into their daily routines, they made visible the tensions, commitments, and shared stakes that hold teams together. Their openness made it possible to see how meaning is built through the everyday work of teams.

I am grateful to Meredith Norwich at Routledge, who saw potential in my early book proposal. Her guidance sharpened both the argument and its accessibility.

Finally, I thank my wife, Doreen Lee, my most constant teammate. She listened through drafts and frustrations, helping steady the tempo of a project long in the making. And to my children, Ellis and Reed: you continually rewrite the scripts of our family life, reminding me that teams are never fixed but always adapting. Watching you grow has been the most joyful lesson in how shared lives evolve and how meaning is made and remade over time.

Index

For Product Safety Concerns and Information please contact our EU representative GPSR@taylorandfrancis.com
Taylor & Francis Verlag GmbH, Kaufingerstraße 24, 80331 München, Germany

www.ingramcontent.com/pod-product-compliance
Ingram Content Group UK Ltd.
Pitfield, Milton Keynes, MK11 3LW, UK
UKHW022018180926
475701UK00005B/906
9781041315780